In easy steps is an imprint of In Easy Steps Limited
16 Hamilton Terrace · Holly Walk · Leamington Spa
Warwickshire · United Kingdom · CV32 4LY
www.ineasysteps.com

Notice of Liability
Every effort has been made to ensure that this book contains accurate
and current information. However, In Easy Steps Limited and the
author shall not be liable for any loss or damage suffered by readers
as a result of any information contained herein.

Trademarks
OS X® is a registered trademark of Apple Computer, Inc. All other
trademarks are acknowledged as belonging to their respective
companies.

In Easy Steps Limited supports The Forest Stewardship Council (FSC),
the leading international forest certification organization. All our titles
that are printed on Greenpeace approved FSC certified paper carry the
FSC logo.

MIX
Paper from
responsible sources
FSC® C020837

Printed and bound in the United Kingdom

ISBN 978-1-84078-695-8

Contents

4   Navigating in OS X El Capitan   75

5   OS X El Capitan Apps   95

6   Getting Productive   107

1 Introducing OS X El Capitan

OS X El Capitan is the latest operating system from Apple, for its range of desktop and laptop computers. This chapter introduces OS X El Capitan and shows how to install it and get started using its wide array of features.

UNIX is an operating system that has traditionally been used for large commercial mainframe computers. It is renowned for its stability and ability to be used within different computing environments.

The New icon pictured above indicates a new or enhanced feature introduced with the latest version of OS X – El Capitan.

About OS X El Capitan

OS X El Capitan is the eleventh version (10.11) of the operating system for Apple computers; the iMac, MacBook, Mac Mini and Mac Pro. When OS X (pronounced 'ten') was first introduced it was a major breakthrough in terms of ease of use and stability. It is based on the UNIX programming language, which is a very stable and secure operating environment and ensures that OS X is one of the most stable consumer operating systems that has ever been designed. More importantly for the user, it is also one of the most stylish and user-friendly operating systems available.

Through the previous 10 versions of OS X, it has been refined and improved in terms of both performance and functionality. This process continues with OS X El Capitan, which further develops the innovations introduced by its two immediate predecessors, OS X Yosemite and OS X Mountain Lion.

When OS X Mountain Lion was introduced, in 2012, it contained a range of innovative functions that were inspired by Apple's mobile devices: iPhone, iPad and iPod Touch. This was continued with the next version of the operating system, OS X Yosemite, and now OS X El Capitan. The two main areas where the functionality of the mobile devices has been transferred to the desktop and laptop operating system are:

- The way apps can be downloaded and installed. Instead of using a disc, OS X El Capitan utilizes the App Store to provide apps, which can be installed in a couple of steps.

- Options for navigating around pages and applications on a trackpad or a Magic Mouse. Instead of having to use a mouse or a traditional laptop trackpad, OS X El Capitan allows Multi-Touch Gestures that provide a range of ways for accessing apps and web pages and navigating around them.

OS X El Capitan continues the evolution of the operating system, by adding more features and enhancing the ones that were already there. This includes greater functionality for full screen mode in various apps; Split View for improved productivity by being able to view two windows next to each other; added functions for the Notes app; the introduction of transit options for the Maps app; and the availability of Apple Music, the subscription music service from Apple. OS X El Capitan also continues the development of iCloud for backing up and sharing content from your Mac.

Installing OS X El Capitan

When it comes to installing OS X El Capitan you do not need to worry about an installation CD or DVD; it can be downloaded and installed directly from the online App Store. New Macs will have OS X El Capitan installed and the following range is compatible with OS X El Capitan and can be upgraded with it:

- iMac (Mid 2007 or newer)

- MacBook (Late 2008 Aluminum, or Early 2009 or newer)

- MacBook Pro (Mid/Late 2007 or newer)

- MacBook Air (Late 2008 or newer)

- Mac Mini (Early 2009 or newer)

- Mac Pro (Early 2008 or newer)

If you want to install OS X El Capitan on an existing Mac, you will need to have the minimum requirements of:

- OS X Snow Leopard (version 10.6.8), OS X Lion, OS X Mountain Lion, OS X Mavericks or OS X Yosemite

- Intel Core 2 Duo, Core i3, Core i5, Core i7, or Xeon processor, or higher

- 2GB of memory and 8GB of available storage for installation

If your Mac meets these requirements, you can download and install OS X El Capitan, for free, as follows:

OS X El Capitan is a free upgrade from the App Store if you already have the Snow Leopard, Lion, Mountain Lion, Mavericks or Yosemite versions of OS X.

1 Click on this icon on the Dock to access the App Store (or select **Software Update**, see tip)

2 Locate the **OS X El Capitan** icon (this will be on the **Featured** page or within the **Productivity** category)

OS X El Capitan
Utilities
DOWNLOAD ▼

3 Click on the **Download** button and follow the installation instructions

To check your computer's software version and upgrade options, click on **Apple menu > About This Mac** from the main Menu bar. See page 12 for details.

The OS X Environment

The first most noticeable element about OS X is its elegant user interface. This has been designed to create a user friendly graphic overlay to the UNIX operating system at the heart of OS X and it is a combination of rich colors and sharp, original graphics. The main elements that make up the initial OS X environment are:

Hot tip

The Dock is designed to help make organizing and opening items as quick and easy as possible. For a detailed look at the Dock, see Chapter Two.

Apple menu   Menu bar   Windows   Menu bar icons

The Dock   Desktop

Don't forget

Many of the behind-the-scenes features of OS X El Capitan are aimed at saving power on your Mac. These include time coalescing technologies for saving processing and battery power, features for saving energy when apps are not being used; power saving features in Safari for ignoring additional content provided by web page plug-ins and memory compression to make your Mac quicker and more responsive.

The **Apple menu** is standardized throughout OS X, regardless of the app in use

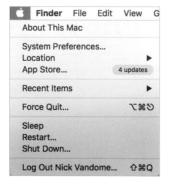

Menus

Menus in OS X contain commands for the operating system and any relevant apps. If there is an arrow next to a command it means there are subsequent options for the item. Some menus also incorporate the same transparency as the sidebar so that the background shows through.

Transparency

One feature in OS X El Capitan is that the sidebar and toolbars in certain apps are transparent so that you can see some of the screen behind it. This also helps the uppermost window blend in with the background:

1 In certain apps with a sidebar, such as the Finder or the Safari sidebar, the background appears behind the sidebar

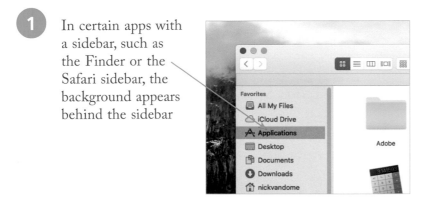

2 When you move the window the background behind the sidebar changes accordingly

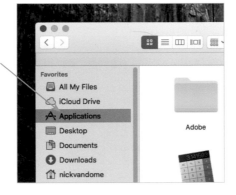

Window buttons

These appear in any open OS X window and can be used to manipulate the window. In OS X El Capitan they include a full screen option. Use the window buttons to, from left to right, close a window, minimize a window or maximize a window.

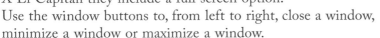

If an app has full screen functionality, this green button is available:

Don't forget

The red window button is used to close a window and in some cases, such as Notes, Reminders and Calendar, it also closes the app. The amber button is used to minimize a window, so that it appears at the right-hand side of the Dock.

About Your Mac

When you buy a new Mac, you will almost certainly check the technical specifications before you make a purchase. Once you have your Mac, there will be times when you will want to view these specifications again, such as the version of OS X in use, the amount of memory and the amount of storage. This can be done through the About This Mac option, which can be accessed from the Apple Menu. To do this:

1 Click on the **Apple Menu** and click on the **About This Mac** link

2 Click on the **Overview** tab

3 This window contains information about the version of OS X being used, processor, amount of memory, type of graphics card and serial number

The System Report section is also where you can check whether your Mac is compatible with the Handoff functionality, which does not work with most pre-2012 Macs. Click on the **Bluetooth** section in the **System Report** to see if Handoff is supported.

4 Click on the **System Report...** button to view full details about the hardware and software on your Mac

...cont'd

5 Click on the **Software Update...** button to see available software updates for your Mac

Display information

This gives information about your Mac's display:

1 Click on the **Displays** tab

Displays

2 This window contains information about your Mac's display, including the type, size, resolution and graphics card

Built-in Display
13.3-inch (1280 x 800)
Intel HD Graphics 3000 384 MB

Displays Preferences...

For more information about Software Updates, see page 181.

For more information about changing the resolution, see page 18.

13

3 Click on the **Displays Preferences...** button to view options for changing the display's resolution, brightness and color

Displays Preferences...

Built-in Display   Q Search

Display   Color

Resolution: ● Best for display
              ○ Scaled

Brightness: ———————————○——

              ☑ Automatically adjust brightness

☑ Show mirroring options in the menu bar when available

...cont'd

Storage information

This contains information about your Mac's physical and removable storage:

 Click on the **Storage** tab   Storage

 This window contains information about the used and available storage on your hard disk and also options for writing various types of CDs and DVDs

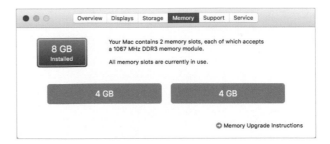

Memory information

This contains information about your Mac's memory, which is used to run OS X and also the applications on your computer:

 Click on the **Memory** tab   Memory

2 This window contains information about the memory chips that are in your Mac

3 Click on the **Memory Upgrade Instructions** if you want to upgrade your memory

4 A page on the Apple website opens, and gives instructions for upgrading memory chips for different makes and models of Macs

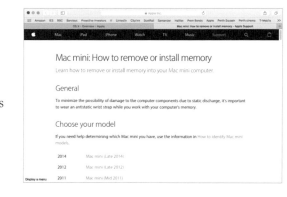

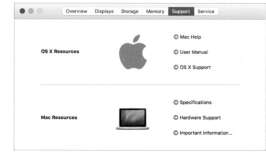

Always wear an anti-static wristband if you are opening your Mac to insert new memory chips, or any other time when you are working on the components of your Mac. This will prevent a build-up of static electricity which could short-circuit the parts and cause permanent damage.

Support

The **Support** tab provides links to a range of help options for your Mac and OS X.

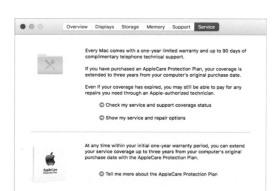

Service

The **Service** tab provides links to service and repair options, and also the AppleCare Protection Plan, for extending the initial one-year warranty for your Mac.

About System Preferences

OS X El Capitan has a wide range of options for customizing and configuring the way that your Mac operates. These are located within the System Preferences section. To access this:

For more detailed information about the Dock, see Chapter Two.

For a detailed look at the System Preferences, see pages 34-35.

 Click on this button on the Dock (the bar of icons that appears along the bottom of the screen), or from the Applications folder

 All of the options are shown in the **System Preferences** window

3 Click once on an item to open it in the main System Preferences window. Each item will have a number of options for customization

4 Click on the **Show All** button to return to the main System Preferences window

Changing the Appearance

The general appearance of items within OS X El Capitan can be changed within the General System Preferences. This includes the color of buttons, menus and windows, highlight colors and the size of icons in the sidebar. To make these changes:

1 Click on this button in the **System Preferences** folder

2 The default options are displayed

3 Click here to select a color for buttons, menus and windows

4 Click here to select a highlight color for items

5 Click here for options for the scroll bars in OS X El Capitan

6 The general appearance of OS X El Capitan can be customized to your own style

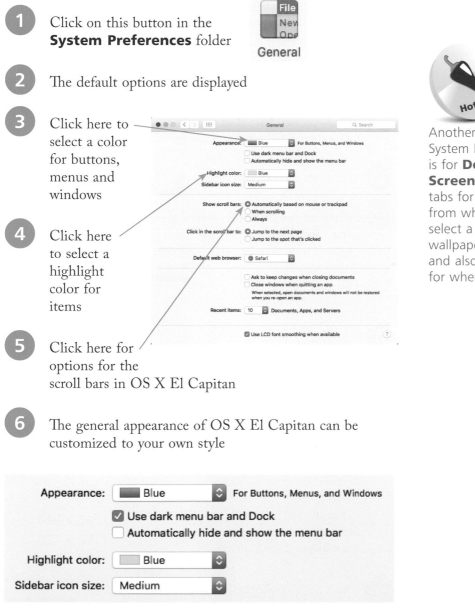

Hot tip

Another option in System Preferences is for **Desktop & Screensaver**. This has tabs for these items, from which you can select a background wallpaper for your Mac and also a screensaver for when it is inactive.

17

Changing the Resolution

For most computer users the size at which items are displayed on the screen is a crucial issue: if items are too small this can make them hard to read and lead to eye strain; too large and you have to spend a lot of time scrolling around to see everything.

The size of items on the screen is controlled by the screen's resolution, i.e. the number of colored dots displayed in an area of the screen. The higher the resolution, the smaller the items on the screen; the lower the resolution, the larger the items. To change the screen resolution:

Don't forget

A higher resolution makes items appear sharper on the screen, even though they appear physically smaller.

18

1 Click on this button in the **System Preferences** folder

Displays

2 Click on the **Display** tab

Display

3 Click on the **Best for display** button to let your Mac select the most appropriate resolution

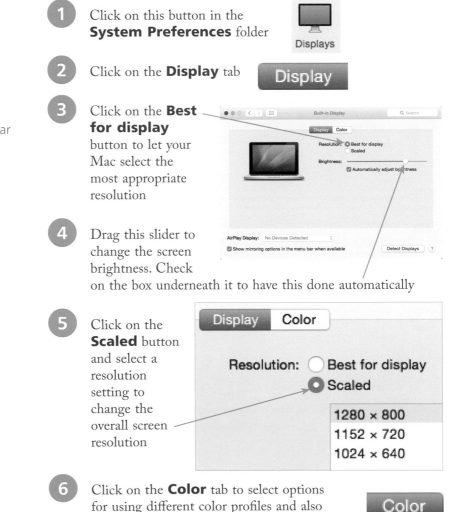

4 Drag this slider to change the screen brightness. Check on the box underneath it to have this done automatically

5 Click on the **Scaled** button and select a resolution setting to change the overall screen resolution

Display	Color

Resolution: ○ Best for display
● Scaled

1280 × 800
1152 × 720
1024 × 640

6 Click on the **Color** tab to select options for using different color profiles and also calibrating your monitor

Color

Accessibility

In all areas of computing it is important to give as many people access to the system as possible. This includes users with visual impairments and also people who have problems using the mouse and keyboard. In OS X this is achieved through the functions of the Accessibility System Preferences. To use these:

1 Click on this button in the **System Preferences** folder

2 Click on the **Display** button for options to change the display colors, contrast and increase the cursor size

3 Click on the **Zoom** button for options to zoom in on the screen

4 Click on the **VoiceOver** button to enable VoiceOver, which provides a spoken description of what is on the screen

Experiment with the VoiceOver function, if only to see how it operates. This will give you a better idea of how visually impaired users access information on a computer.

In OS X El Capitan, the VoiceOver function has support for iBooks.

...cont'd

 5 Click on
the **Audio**
button to
select an on-
screen flash
for alerts and
how sound is
played

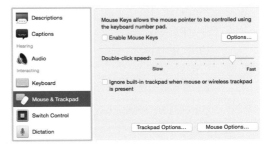

The Audio, Keyboard
and Mouse & Trackpad
accessibility options
have links to additional
options within their own
System Preferences.

6 Click on the
Keyboard
button
to access
options for
customizing
the keyboard

Another option in the
Accessibility window is
for **Switch Control**,
which enables a Mac to
be controlled by a variety
of devices, including
the mouse, keypad and
gamepad devices.

7 Click on the
**Mouse &
Trackpad**
button
to access
options for
customizing
these devices

8 Click on the
Dictation
button to
select options
for using
spoken
commands

The Spoken Word

OS X El Capitan not only has numerous options for adding text to documents, emails and messages; it also has a dictation function so that you can speak what you want to appear on screen. To set up and use the dictation feature:

1 Click on this button in the **System Preferences** folder

Dictation & Speech

2 By default, Dictation is **Off**

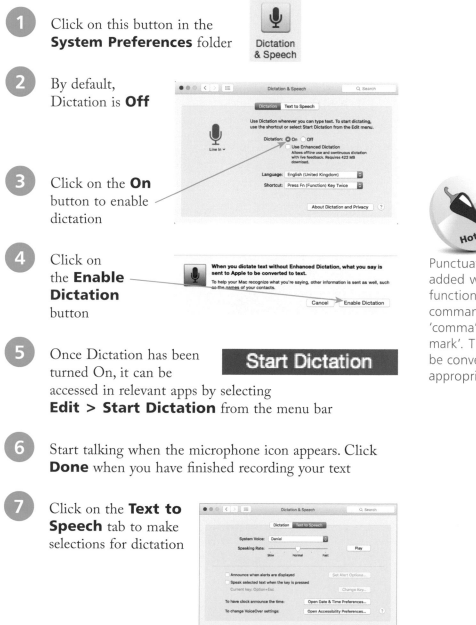

3 Click on the **On** button to enable dictation

4 Click on the **Enable Dictation** button

5 Once Dictation has been turned On, it can be accessed in relevant apps by selecting **Edit > Start Dictation** from the menu bar

Start Dictation

6 Start talking when the microphone icon appears. Click **Done** when you have finished recording your text

7 Click on the **Text to Speech** tab to make selections for dictation

21

Hot tip

Punctuation can be added with the dictation function, by speaking commands such as 'comma' or 'question mark'. These will then be converted into the appropriate symbols.

When shutting down, make sure you have saved all of your open documents, although OS X will prompt you to do this if you have forgotten.

OS X El Capitan has a **Resume** function where your Mac opens up in the same state as when you shut it down. See page 50 for details.

Shutting Down

The Apple menu (which can be accessed by clicking on the Apple icon at the top left corner of the Desktop or any subsequent OS X window) has been standardized in OS X. This means that it has the same options regardless of the app in which you are working. This has a number of advantages, not least is the fact that it makes it easier to shut down your Mac. When shutting down, there are three options that can be selected:

- **Sleep**. This puts the Mac into hibernation mode, i.e. the screen goes blank and the hard drive becomes inactive. This state is maintained until the mouse is moved or a key is pressed on the keyboard. This then wakes up the Mac and it is ready to continue work.

- **Restart**. This closes down the Mac and then restarts it again. This can be useful if you have added new software and your computer requires a restart to make it active.

- **Shut Down**. This closes down the Mac completely once you have finished working.

Click here to access the **Apple menu**

	Finder	File	Edit	View	G
About This Mac
System Preferences...
Location ▶
App Store...	4 updates
Recent Items ▶
Force Quit... ⌥⌘⍈
Sleep
Restart...
Shut Down...
Log Out Nick Vandome... ⇧⌘Q

Click here to access one of the shut down options

2 Getting Up and Running

This chapter looks at some of the essential features of OS X El Capitan. These include the Dock for organizing and accessing all of the elements of your Mac computer, the System Preferences for the way your Mac looks and operates and items for arranging folders and files. It also introduces the online sharing service, iCloud, for sharing your digital content, including the Family Sharing feature for sharing your photos, music, apps and books with family members.

The Dock is always displayed as a line of icons, but this can be orientated either vertically or horizontally.

Items on the Dock can be opened by clicking on them once, rather than having to double-click on them. Once they have been accessed, the icon bobs up and down until the item is available.

The Downloads icon can be displayed as a Folder or a Stack (see pages 28-29). To set this, Ctrl + click on the Download icon and select either **Folder** or **Stack** under the **Display as** option.

Introducing the Dock

The Dock is one of the main organizational elements of OS X. Its main function is to help organize and access apps, folders and files. In addition, with its redesigned background and icons, it also makes an aesthetically pleasing addition to the Desktop. The main things to remember about the Dock are:

● It is divided into two: apps go on the left of the dividing line; all other items go on the right.

● It can be customized in several different ways.

By default, the Dock appears at the bottom of the screen

Apps go here   Dividing line   Open items

By default, the two icons to the right of the dividing line are:

Downloads. This is for items that you have downloaded from the web. The items can be accessed from here and opened or run.

Trash. This is where items can be dragged to if you want to remove them. It can also be used to eject removable discs, such as pen drives, by dragging the device's icon over the Trash. It cannot be removed from the Dock.

Apps on the Dock

Opening apps

When you open apps they appear on the Dock and can be worked within the Dock environment.

1 Click once on an app to open it (either on the Dock, the Finder Applications folder or the Launchpad). Once an app has been opened it is displayed on the Dock, with a black dot underneath it

2 When windows are opened within the app these are displayed to the right of the dividing line

3 Click on an icon to the right of the dividing line to maximize it: it disappears from the Dock and displays at full size

4 If a window is minimized by clicking on this button, it goes back to the right-hand side of the dividing line on the Dock

5 Press and hold underneath an open app to view the available windows for the app (this will differ for different apps as some operate by using a single window)

```
Weekly budgets
♦ Weekly budgets
  Options          ▶
  Show All Windows
  Hide
  Quit
```

6 To close an open app, press and hold underneath its icon on the Dock and click on the **Quit** button (or select its name on the Menu bar and select **Quit**)

```
Show All Windows
Hide
Quit
```

Apps can be opened from the Dock, the Finder or the Launchpad. The Finder is covered in detail in Chapter Three, and see pages 96-97 for more on the Launchpad.

Some apps, such as Notes, Reminders and Calendar, will close when the active window is closed. Others, such as Pages, Keynote and Numbers, will remain open even if all of the windows are closed: the recently-accessed documents will be displayed as in Step 5.

Setting Dock Preferences

As with most elements of OS X, the Dock can be modified in numerous ways. This can affect both the appearance of the Dock and the way it operates. To set Dock preferences:

Hot tip

The Apple menu is constantly available in OS X, regardless of the app in which you are working. The menu options are also constant in all apps.

Beware

The Dock cannot be moved by dragging it physically; this can only be done in the Dock Preferences window.

Beware

You cannot make the Dock size so large that some of the icons would not be visible on the Desktop. By default, the Dock is resized so that everything is always visible.

1 Select **System Preferences > Dock**

Dock

2 The Dock Preferences allow you to change its size, orientation, the way icons appear and effects for when items are minimized

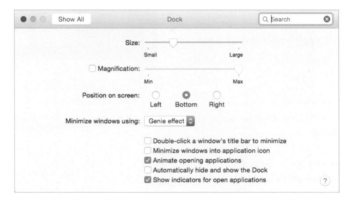

Drag the Dock **Size** slider to increase or decrease the size of the Dock

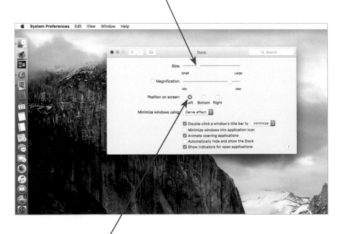

The **Position on screen** options enable you to place the Dock on the left, right or bottom of the screen

Check on the **Magnification** box and drag the slider to determine the size to which icons are enlarged when the cursor is moved over them

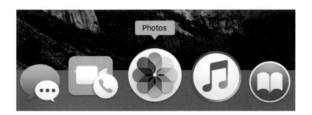

Move the cursor over an icon on the Dock to see the magnification effect.

Open windows can also be minimized by double-clicking on their title bar (the thinly lined bar at the top of the window, next to the three window buttons).

The **Genie effect** under the **Minimize windows using** option shrinks the item to be minimized like a genie going back into its lamp

Manual resizing
In addition to changing the size of the Dock by using the Dock Preference dialog box, it can also be resized manually:

Drag vertically on the Dock dividing line to increase or decrease its size

Stacks on the Dock

Stacking items

To save space, it is possible to add folders to the Dock, where their contents can easily be accessed. This is known as Stacks. By default, Stacks for documents and downloaded files are created on the Dock. To use Stacks:

Don't forget

When the cursor is moved over an item in the Dock, the name of that item is displayed above it.

 Stacked items are placed on the right of the Dock dividing line

 Click on a Stack to view its contents

 Stacks can be viewed as a grid, or

Hot tip

To create a new Stack, drag a folder to the right-hand side of the Dock, i.e. to the right of the dividing line.

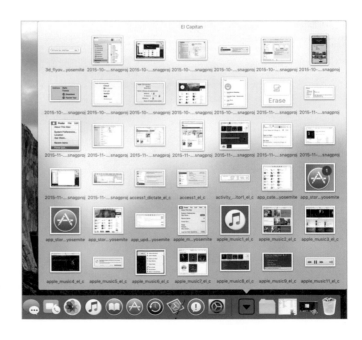

4 As a fan, depending on the number of items it contains, or

Hot tip

Move the cursor over a stack and press Ctrl (key) + click to access options for how that stack is displayed.

5 As a list. Click on a folder to view its contents within a Stack, then click on files to open them in their relevant app

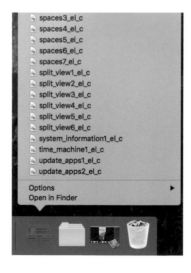

6 To create a new Stack, drag a folder onto the Dock. Any new items that are added to the folder will also be visible through the Stack

Dock Menus

One of the features of the Dock is that it can display contextual menus for selected items. This means that it shows menus with options that are applicable to the item that is being accessed. This can only be done when an item has been opened.

1 Click and hold here to display an item's individual menu

Click on Quit on the Dock's contextual menu to close an open app or file, depending on which side of the dividing bar the item is located.

2 Click on **Show in Finder** to see where the item is located on your computer

Working with Dock Items

Adding items

As many items as you like can be added to the Dock; the only restriction is the size of monitor in which to display all of the Dock items (the size of the Dock can be reduced to accommodate more icons but you have to be careful that all of the icons are still legible). To add items to the Dock:

 Locate the required item and drag it onto the Dock. All of the other icons move along to make space for the new one

Don't forget

Icons on the Dock are shortcuts to the related item, rather than the item itself, which remains in its original location.

31

Keep in Dock

Every time you open a new app, its icon will appear in the Dock for the duration that the program is open, even if it has not previously been put in the Dock. If you then decide that you would like to keep it in the Dock, you can do so as follows:

Beware

You can add numerous items to the Dock, but it will automatically shrink to display all of its items if it becomes too big for the available space.

 Click and hold on the button below an open app

2 Select **Options > Keep In Dock** to ensure the app remains in the Dock when it is closed

...cont'd

Removing items

Any item, except the Finder, can be removed from the Dock. However, this does not remove it from your computer, it just removes the shortcut for accessing it. You will still be able to locate it in its folder on your hard drive and, if required, drag it back onto the Dock. To remove items from the Dock:

 Drag the item away from the Dock until it displays the **Remove** tag. The item disappears once the cursor is released. All of the other icons then move up to fill in the space

Removing open apps

You can remove an app from the Dock, even if it is open and running. To do this:

Hot tip

When an icon is dragged from the Dock, it has to be moved a reasonable distance before the Remove alert appears.

 Drag an app off the Dock while it is running. Initially the icon will remain on the Dock because the app is still open

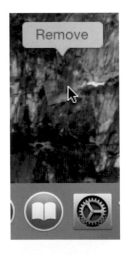

 When the app is closed its icon will be removed from the Dock (unless **Keep in Dock** has been selected from the item's Dock menu)

Trash

The Trash folder is a location for placing items that you do not want to use anymore. However, when items are placed in the Trash, they are not removed from your computer. This requires another command, as the Trash is really a holding area before you decide you want to remove items permanently. The Trash can also be used for ejecting removable disks attached to your Mac.

Sending items to the Trash
Items can be sent to the Trash by dragging them from the location in which they are stored.

Items can also be sent to the Trash by selecting them and then selecting **File > Move to Trash** from the Menu bar.

 Drag an item over the **Trash** icon to place it in the Trash folder

2 Click once on the **Trash** icon on the Dock to view its contents

All of the items within the Trash can be removed in a single command: Select **Finder > Empty Trash** from the Menu bar to remove all of the items in the Trash folder.

System Preferences

In OS X there are preferences that can be set for just about every aspect of the app. This gives you greater control over how the interface looks and how the operating system functions. To access System Preferences:

 Click on this icon on the Dock or from the Applications folder in the Finder

Personal preferences

General. Options for the overall look of buttons, menus, windows and scroll bars.

Desktop & Screen Saver. This can be used to change the Desktop background and the screen saver.

Dock. Options for the way the Dock looks and functions.

Mission Control. This gives you a variety of options for managing all of your open windows and apps.

Language & Region. Options for the language used on your Mac.

Security & Privacy. This enables you to secure your Home folder with a master password, for added security.

Spotlight. This can be used to specify settings for the OS X search facility, Spotlight.

Notifications. This can be used to set up how you are notified about items such as email, messages and software updates.

Hardware preferences

CDs & DVDs. Options for what action is taken when you insert CDs and DVDs.

Displays. Options for the screen display, such as resolution.

Energy Saver. Options for when the computer is inactive.

Keyboard. Options for how the keyboard functions and also keyboard shortcuts.

Mouse. Options for how the mouse functions.

Trackpad. Options for if you are using a trackpad.

Printers & Scanners. Options for selecting printers and scanners.

Don't forget

OS X El Capitan supports multiple displays, which means you can connect your Mac to two or more displays and view different content on each one. The Dock appears on the active screen and each screen also has its own menu bar. Different full screen apps can also be viewed on each screen.

...cont'd

Sound. Options for adding sound effects and playing and recording sound.

Internet & Wireless preferences
iCloud. Options for the online iCloud service.

Internet Accounts. This can be used to set up contacts on your Mac, using a variety of online services.

Extensions. This can be used to customize your Mac with extensions and plugins from Apple and third-party developers.

Network. This can be used to specify network settings for linking two or more computers together.

Bluetooth. Options for attaching Bluetooth wireless devices.

Sharing. This can be used to specify how files are shared over a network. This is also covered in Chapter 10.

System preferences
Users & Groups. This can be used to allow different users to create their own accounts for use on the same computer.

Parental Controls. This can be used to limit access to the computer and various online functions.

App Store. This can be used to specify how software updates are handled. It connects to the App Store to access the available updates.

Dictation & Speech. Options for using speakable commands to control the computer.

Date & Time. Options for changing the computer's date and time, to time zones around the world.

Startup Disk. This can be used to specify the disk from which your computer starts up. This is usually the OS X volume.

Time Machine. This can be used to configure and set up the OS X backup facility.

Accessibility. This can be used to set options for users who have difficulty with viewing text on screen, hearing commands, using the keyboard or using the mouse.

The **Internet Accounts** section can be used to set up email accounts and also link to your social networking accounts such as Facebook, Twitter and LinkedIn.

About iCloud

Cloud computing is an attractive proposition and one that has gained greatly in popularity in recent years. As a concept, it consists of storing your content on an external computer server. This not only gives you added security in terms of backing up your information, it also means that the content can then be shared over a variety of mobile devices.

iCloud is Apple's consumer cloud computing product that consists of online services such as email, a calendar, notes, contacts and saving documents. iCloud provides users with a way to save and backup their files and content to the online service and then use them across their Apple devices such as other Mac computers, iPhones, iPads and iPod Touches.

About iCloud
iCloud can be set up from this icon within System Preferences:

You can use iCloud to save and share the following between your different devices, with an Apple ID account.

- Music
- Photos
- Documents
- Apps
- Books
- Backups
- Contacts, Calendar, Notes and Reminders

When you save an item to the iCloud it automatically pushes it to all of your other compatible devices; you do not have to manually sync anything, iCloud does it all for you.

The standard iCloud service is free and this includes an iCloud email address and 5GB of online storage. (*Correct at the time of printing.*)

There is also a version of iCloud for Windows, which can be accessed for download from the Apple website at **www.apple.com/ icloud/setup/pc.html**

Setting up iCloud

To use iCloud with OS X El Capitan you need to first have an Apple ID. This is a service you can register for to be able to access a range of Apple facilities, including iCloud. You can register with an email address and a password. When you first start using iCloud you will be prompted for your Apple ID details. If you do not have an Apple ID you can apply for one at this point.

1 Sign in with your Apple ID, or

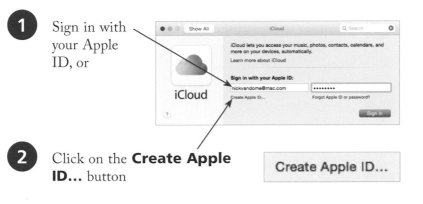

When you have an Apple ID and an iCloud account, you can also use the iCloud website to access your content. Access the website at **www.icloud.com** and log in with your Apple ID details.

2 Click on the **Create Apple ID...** button

Setting up iCloud
To use iCloud:

1 Open System Preferences and click on the **iCloud** button

2 Check on the items you want included within iCloud. All of these items will be backed up and shared across all of your Apple devices

The online iCloud service includes your online email service, Contacts, Calendar, Reminders, Notes and versions of Pages, Keynote and Numbers. You can log in to your iCloud account from any internet-enabled device.

About the iCloud Drive

One of the options in the iCloud section is for the iCloud Drive. This can be used to store documents and other content so that you can use them on any other Apple devices that you have, such as an iPhone or an iPad. With the iCloud Drive you can start work on a document on one device and continue on another device from where you left off. To set up the iCloud Drive:

1 Click on the **iCloud** button in System Preferences

2 Check **On** the **iCloud Drive** option and click on the **Options...** button

3 Select the apps that you want to use with the iCloud Drive

Pages is the Apple app for word processing, Numbers for spreadsheets and Keynote for presentations. These can all be downloaded from the App Store.

4 Click on the **Done** button

Using the iCloud Drive

To work with files in the iCloud Drive:

1 In the Finder sidebar click on the **iCloud Drive** button

2 Certain iCloud Drive folders are already created, based on the apps that you have selected on the previous page. These are the default folders into which content from their respective apps will be placed (although others can also be selected, if required). Double-click on a folder to view its contents

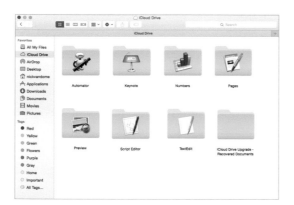

3 To save files into an iCloud Drive folder, select **File > Save As** from the Menu bar, click on the **iCloud Drive** button in the Finder sidebar and navigate to the required folder for the file

Hot tip

Another useful iCloud function is the iCloud Keychain (**System Preferences > iCloud** and check on the **Keychain** option). If this is enabled, it can keep all of your passwords and credit card information up-to-date across multiple devices and remember them when you use them on websites. The information is encrypted and controlled through your Apple ID.

39

Continuity

One of the main themes of OS X El Capitan, and iOS 8 (and later) for mobile devices, is to make all of your content available on all of your Apple devices. This is known as Continuity: when you create something on one device you can then pick it up and finish it on another. This is done through iCloud. To do this:

 Ensure the app has iCloud activated, as on page 37

 Create the content in the app on your Mac

Open the same app on another Apple device, e.g. an iPad. The item created on your Mac should be available to view and edit. Any changes will then show up on the file on your Mac too

It is also possible to continue an email with the Continuity feature. First, create it on your Mac and then close it. You will be prompted to save the email as a draft and, if you do this, you will be able to open it from the **Drafts** mailbox on another Apple device.

Handoff

Handoff is one of the key features of Continuity and it displays icons of items that you have opened on another device, such as Safari web pages. Handoff does not work with all devices and it only works if both devices have OS X Yosemite (or later) and iOS 8 (or later), for mobile devices.

Handoff has had some teething problems and it sometimes takes a bit of trial and error to make it work properly. To use Handoff you will need to do the following:

- Your Mac must be running OS X Yosemite (or later) and your mobile device (iPhone 5 and later, iPad 4 and later, all models of iPad mini and the 5th generation iPod Touch) must have iOS 8 (or later).

- Your Mac has to support Bluetooth 4.0, which means that most pre-2012 Macs are not compatible with Handoff.

- To check if your Mac supports Handoff, select **Apple Menu > About This Mac > System Report**. Click on **Bluetooth** to see if Handoff is supported.

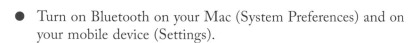

Bluetooth Low Energy Supported:	Yes
Handoff Supported:	Yes
Instant Hotspot Supported:	Yes

- Turn on Bluetooth on your Mac (System Preferences) and on your mobile device (Settings).

- Turn on Handoff on your Mac (**System Preferences > General** and check on **Allow Handoff Between this Mac and your iCloud Devices**) and on your mobile device (**Settings > General > Handoff & Suggested Apps**).

- When Handoff is activated, compatible apps will be displayed at the left-hand side of the Dock when they have been opened on another device.

Don't forget

The apps that work with Handoff are Mail, Safari, Maps, Messages, Reminders, Calendar, Contacts, Notes, Pages, Numbers and Keynote.

41

Beware

Handoff does not always work perfectly, even between compatible devices. If it is not working, try turning both devices off and on and do the same with Bluetooth. Also, try logging out, and then back in, of your iCloud account on both devices.

About Family Sharing

As everyone gets more and more digital devices it is becoming increasingly important to be able to share content with other people, particularly family members. In OS X El Capitan, and iCloud, the Family Sharing function enables you to share items that you have downloaded from the App Store, such as music and movies, with up to six other family members, as long as they have an Apple ID. Once this has been set up it is also possible to share items such as family calendars, photos and even see where family members' devices are located. To set up Family Sharing:

Don't forget

To use Family Sharing, other family members must have an Apple device using either iOS 8 (or later) for a mobile device (iPad, iPhone or iPod Touch) or OS X Yosemite (or later) for a desktop or laptop Mac computer.

1 Click on the **iCloud** button in System Preferences

iCloud

2 Click on the **Set Up Family Sharing** (or the **Manage Family** button if Family Sharing has already been set up)

3 One person will be the organizer of Family Sharing, i.e. in charge of it, and if

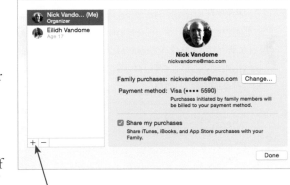

you set it up then it will be you. Click on the **+** button to add other family members

4 Enter
the
name
or email
address
of a
family
member

Add a family member

● Enter a family member's name or email address.

Lucy Vandome <lavme@hotmail.co.uk>

○ Create an Apple ID for a child who doesn't have an account.

Cancel   Continue

and click on the **Continue** button

5 Verify your
debit or
credit card
information
for your
iCloud
account,

Verify the security code on your card.

This payment method will be used to pay for purchases initiated by your family members.

Security code for Visa (•••• ▮): ▮

Go Back   Continue

as this will be used by the family member for making purchases. Click on the **Continue** button

6 Enter your
Apple ID
password
and click
on the
Continue
button

Enter your password to make changes to your account.

null

Password: •••••••   Forgot?

Cancel   Continue

7 An
invitation
is sent
to the
selected
person.
They
have to
accept
this
before

Nick Vando... (Me)
Organizer

Eilidh Vandome
Age 17

Lucy Vandome
Invitation sent

LV

Lucy Vandome
lavme@hotmail.co.uk

Lucy has not yet accepted your invitation.

Resend Invitation

+ −

Done

they can participate in Family Sharing

Beware

If children are part of the Family Sharing group you can specify that they need your permission before downloading any items from the iTunes Store, the App Store or the iBooks Store. To do this, click on **iCloud** in **System Preferences** and click on the **Manage Family** button. Select a family member and check **On** the **Ask to Buy** button. You will then receive a notification whenever they want to buy something and you can either allow or deny their request.

Using Family Sharing

Once Family Sharing has been set up it can be used by members of the group to share music, apps, movies and books. There is also a shared Family calendar that can be used, and it is also possible to view the location of the devices of the family members.

Sharing music

To share music, and other content from the iTunes Store, such as movies and TV shows:

1 Click on the **iTunes** app on the Dock

2 Click on the **Purchased** link

MUSIC QUICK LINKS

Redeem   Account
Send iTunes Gifts   Support

Purchased

3 By default, your own purchases are displayed. Click on the **Purchased** button to view other members of Family Sharing

Purchased Nick ⌄

4 Click on another family member to view their purchases (they will be able to do this for your purchases too)

Purchased

✓ 🧑 Nick

🔍 Search Purchased Items

👩 Eilidh

5 Click on the iCloud button to download the other family member's music tracks or albums

Purchased Eilidh ⌄

🔍 Search Purchased Items

All Albums
U2

Songs of Innocence
U2

Sharing apps

Apps can also be shared from the App Store. To do this:

1 Click on the **App Store** app on the Dock

2 Click on the **Purchases** button

3 By default, your own purchases are displayed. Click on the **My Purchases** button to view other members of Family Sharing

4 Click on another family member to view and download their purchased apps (they will be able to do this for your apps too)

Sharing books

Books can also be shared in a similar way to items from the iTunes Store and the App Store. To do this:

1 Click on the **iBooks** app on the Dock

2 Click on the **iBooks Store** button

3 Click on the **Purchased** link

QUICK LINKS

Account

Purchased

4 By default, your own purchases are displayed. Click on the **Purchased** button to view other members of Family Sharing and any books they have downloaded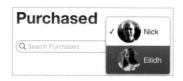

More than one family member can use content in the Family Sharing group at the same time.

...cont'd

Sharing calendars

Family Sharing also generates a Family calendar that can be used by all Family Sharing members:

 Open the **Calendar** app

 Click and hold on a date to create a **New Event**. The current calendar (shown in the top right-hand corner) will probably not be the Family one. Click on this button to change the calendar

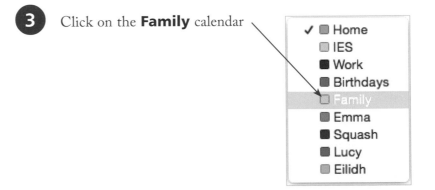

 Click on the **Family** calendar

✓ ■ Home
☐ IES
■ Work
■ Birthdays
☐ Family
■ Emma
■ Squash
■ Lucy
☐ Eilidh

Complete the details for the event. It will be added to your calendar, with the Family color tag. Other people in your Family Sharing circle will have this event added to their Family calendar too and they will be sent a notification

21
• Bowling   17:00

Don't forget

Other members of the Family Sharing group can add items to the Family calendar and, when they do, you will be sent a notification that appears on your Mac.

...cont'd

Finding lost family devices

Family Sharing also makes it possible to see where everyone's devices are, which can be useful for locating people, but particularly so if a device belonging to a Family Sharing member is lost or stolen. To do this:

1 Ensure that the **Find My Mac** function is turned on in the **iCloud** System Preferences, and log in to your online iCloud account at **www.icloud.com**

2 Click on the **Find My iPhone** button (this works for other Apple devices too)

3 Devices that are turned on, online and with iCloud activated are shown by green dots

Don't forget

The location of devices is shown on a map and you can zoom in on the map to see their location more accurately.

4 Click on a green dot to display information about the device. Click on the **i** symbol to access options for managing the device remotely

Eilidh's iPad
Less than a minute ago
Kirkliston   Edinburgh

5 There are options to send an alert sound to the device, lock it remotely or erase its contents (if you are concerned about it having fallen into the wrong hands)

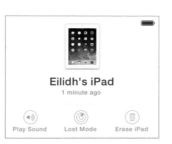

Eilidh's iPad
1 minute ago
Play Sound   Lost Mode   Erase iPad

Desktop Items

If required, the Desktop can be used to store apps and files. However, the Finder (see Chapter Three) does such a good job of organizing all of the elements within your computer that the Desktop is rendered largely redundant, unless you feel happier storing items here. The Desktop can also display any removable disks that are connected to your computer:

Hot tip

Icons for removable disks, e.g. pen drives, CDs or DVDs, will only become visible on the Desktop once a disk has been inserted into the appropriate drive.

If a removable disk is connected to your computer, double-click the desktop icon to view its contents

Don't forget

Any removable disks that are connected to your computer can also be viewed by clicking on them in the Sidebar in the Finder.

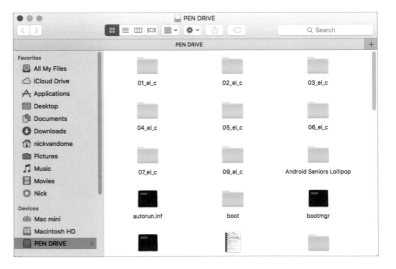

Ejecting Items

If you have removable disks attached to your Mac it is essential to be able to eject them quickly and easily. In OS X there are two ways in which this can be done:

 In the Finder, click on the icon to the right of the name of the removable disk

Devices
- 🖥 Mac mini
- 💾 Macintosh HD
- 💽 **PEN DRIVE** ⏏

 On the Desktop, drag the disk icon over the **Trash**. This turns the Trash icon into the **Eject** icon and the disk will be ejected

Hot tip

If the desktop items are not showing, open the Finder and click on **Finder > Preferences** on the top toolbar and click on the **General** tab. Under **Show these items on the Desktop** check on the items you want, including **Hard Disks**, **External Disks** and **CDs, DVDs and iPods**.

3 Some discs, such as CDs and DVDs, are physically ejected when either of these two actions are performed. Other disks, such as pen drives, have to be removed manually once they have been ejected by OS X. If the disk is not ejected first, the following warning message will appear:

Disk Not Ejected Properly
Eject "PEN DRIVE" before disconnecting or turning it off.

Close

Resuming

One of the chores about computing is that when you close down your computer you have to first close down all of your open documents and apps, and then open them all again when you turn your machine back on. However, OS X El Capitan has a feature that allows you to continue working exactly where you left off, even if you turn off your computer. To do this:

 Before you close down, all of your open documents and apps are available (as shown)

 Select the **Shut Down...** or **Restart...** option from the **Apple menu**

Beware

If you have open, unsaved documents you will be prompted to save them before your Mac is closed down.

 Make sure this box is checked on (this will ensure that all of your items will appear as before, once the Mac is closed down and then opened again)

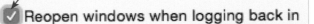
Reopen windows when logging back in

 Confirm the **Shut Down** or **Restart** command

Are you sure you want to shut down your computer now?
If you do nothing, the computer will shut down automatically in 52 seconds.
Reopen windows when logging back in
Cancel   Shut Down

3 Finder

The principal method for moving around OS X El Capitan is the Finder. This enables you to access items and organize your apps, folders and files. This chapter looks at how to use the Finder and how to get the most out of this powerful tool that is at the heart of navigating around OS X. It covers accessing items through the Finder, how to customize the interface and numerous options for working with folders in OS X El Capitan.

Working with the Finder

If you were only able to use one item on the Dock it would be the Finder. This is the gateway to all of the elements of your computer. It is possible to get to selected items through other routes, but the Finder is the only location where you can gain access to everything on your system. If you ever feel that you are getting lost within OS X, click on the Finder and then you should begin to feel more at home. To access the Finder:

1 Click once on this icon on the Dock

Overview

The Finder has its own toolbar; a sidebar from which items can be accessed and a main window where the contents of selected items can be viewed:

A link to the iCloud Drive is also included in the Finder sidebar.

The Actions button has options for displaying information about a selected item and also options for how it is displayed within the Finder.

Forward and back   View options   Actions button   Search

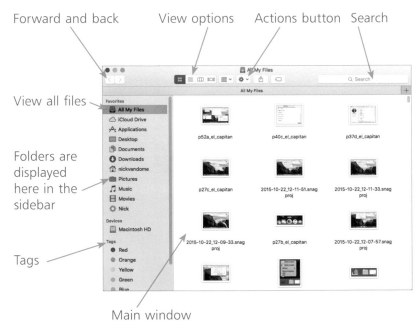

View all files

Folders are displayed here in the sidebar

Tags

Main window

Finder Folders

All My Files

This contains all of the latest files in which you have been working. They are sorted into categories according to file type so that you can search through them quickly. This is an excellent way to locate items without having to look through a lot of folders. To access this:

1 Click on this link in the Finder sidebar to access the contents of your **All My Files** folder

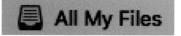

2 All of your files are displayed in individual categories

The Finder is always open (as denoted by the black dot underneath its icon on the Dock) and it cannot readily be closed down or removed.

The Finder sidebar has the OS X El Capitan transparency feature, so that you can see some of the open window, or Desktop, behind it.

All My Files			
Favorites	**Name**	**Date Created** ∨	**Date Last Opened**
All My Files	p55a_el_capitan	Today, 16:37	Today at 16:37
iCloud Drive	2015-10-2...-44.snagproj	Today, 16:36	Today at 16:36
Applications	2015-10-2...-29.snagproj	Today, 16:36	Today at 16:36
Desktop	p54b_el_capitan	Today, 16:35	Today at 16:35
Documents	p52a_el_capitan	Today, 12:23	Today at 12:23
Downloads	p40c_el_capitan	Today, 12:20	Today at 12:20
nickvandome	p37d_el_capitan	Today, 12:17	Today at 12:17
Pictures	p27c_el_capitan	Today, 12:12	Today at 12:12
Music	2015-10-2...-51.snagproj	Today, 12:11	Today at 12:11
Movies	2015-10-2...-33.snagproj	Today, 12:11	Today at 12:11
Nick	2015-10-2...-33.snagproj	Today, 12:09	Today at 12:09
Devices	p27b_el_capitan	Today, 12:08	Today at 12:08
Macintosh HD	2015-10-2...-57.snagproj	Today, 12:07	Today at 12:07
Tags	p26d_el_capitan	Today, 12:07	Today at 12:07
Red	p25d_el_capitan	Today, 12:02	Today at 12:02
Orange	p25b_el_capitan	Today, 12:01	Today at 12:01
Yellow	p24d_el_capitan	Today, 11:57	Today at 11:57
Green	p24c_el_capitan	Today, 11:56	Today at 11:56
Blue	p24a_el_capitan	Today, 11:54	Today at 11:54
	p24b_el_capitan	Today, 11:53	Today at 11:53
	p22a_el_capitan	Today, 11:42	Today at 11:42
	2015-10-2...-15.snagproj	Today, 11:41	Today at 11:41
	p12a_el_capitan	Today, 11:31	Today at 11:31
	2015-10-2...-43.snagproj	Today, 11:30	Today at 11:30
	p11b_el_capitan	Today, 11:30	Today at 11:30

To change the display of folders in the sidebar, click on the **Finder** menu on the top toolbar. Select **Preferences** and click on the **Sidebar** tab. Under **Show these items in the sidebar**, select the items you want included.

3 Click on the headings at the top of each category to sort items by those criteria

...cont'd

Home folder

This contains the contents of your own home directory, containing your personal folders and files. OS X inserts some pre-named folders which it thinks will be useful, but it is possible to rearrange or delete these as you please. It is also possible to add as many more folders as you want.

To delete a folder from the Finder sidebar, Ctrl + click on it and click on **Remove from Sidebar**.

1 Click on this link to access the contents of your **Home** folder

 nickvandome

2 The Home folder contains the **Public** folder that can be used to share files with other users if the computer is part of a network

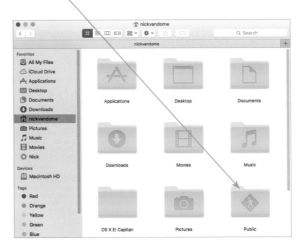

When you are creating documents, OS X by default, recognizes their type and then, when you save them, suggests the most applicable folder in which to save them. If the document is created by an app that is compatible with the iCloud Drive (and iCloud has been activated) then one of the iCloud Drive folders may be selected as the default.

Applications

This folder contains all of the applications on your Mac. They can also be accessed from the Launchpad as shown on page 96.

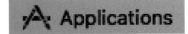

Documents

This is part of your Home folder but is put on the Finder sidebar for ease of access. New folders can be created for different types of documents.

Finder Views

The way in which items are displayed within the Finder can be amended in a variety of ways, depending on how you want to view the contents of a folder. Different folders can have their own viewing options applied to them and these will stay in place until a new option is specified.

Back button

When working within the Finder, each new window replaces the previous one, unless you open a new app. This prevents the screen becoming cluttered with dozens of open windows, as you look through various Finder windows for a particular item. To ensure that you never feel lost within the Finder structure, there is a Back button on the Finder toolbar that enables you to retrace the steps that you have taken.

1 Navigate to a folder within the Finder (in this case the **Malta** folder contained within **Pictures**)

2 Click on the **Back** button to move back to the previously-visited window (in this case, the main **Pictures** window)

Select an item within the Finder window and click on the space bar to view its details.

If you have not opened any Finder windows, the Back button will not operate.

...cont'd

Icon view

One of the viewing options for displaying items within the Finder is as icons. This provides a pictorial representation of the items in the Finder. It is possible to customize the way that Icon view looks and functions.

The **Sort By** options can be used to arrange icons into specific groups, e.g. by name or type, or to snap them to an invisible grid so that they have an ordered appearance.

1 Click here on the Finder toolbar to access **Icon** view

2 Select **View** from the Menu bar, check on **as Icons** and select **Show View Options** to access the options for customizing Icon view

View	Go	Window	Help
✓ as Icons			⌘1
as List			⌘2
as Columns			⌘3
as Cover Flow			⌘4
Clean Up Selection			
Clean Up By			▶
Sort By			▶
Hide Tab Bar			⇧⌘T
Show Path Bar			⌥⌘P
Show Status Bar			⌘/
Hide Sidebar			⌥⌘S
Show Preview			⇧⌘P
Hide Toolbar			⌥⌘T
Customize Toolbar...			
Show View Options			⌘J
Enter Full Screen			^⌘F

A very large icon size can be useful for people with poor eyesight, but it does take up a lot more space in a window.

Drag this slider to set the icon size

Select an option for the way icons are arranged in Finder windows

Select an option for the background of the Finder window

	Pictures
☐ Always open in icon view	
☐ Browse in icon view	
Arrange By:	Name
Sort By:	Name
Icon size: 64 × 64	
A ▬▬▬▬▬▬▬ A	
Grid spacing:	
▦ ▬▬▬▬▬▬▬ ▦	
Text size: 12	
Label position:	
● Bottom ○ Right	
☐ Show item info	
☑ Show icon preview	
Background:	
● White	
○ Color	
○ Picture	
Restore to Defaults	

...cont'd

List view

List view can be used to show the items within a Finder window as a list, with additional information shown next to them. This can be a more efficient method than Icon view if there are a lot of items within a folder, as List view enables you to see more items at one time and also view the additional information.

 Click here on the Finder toolbar to access **List** view

2 The name of each folder or file is displayed here. If any item has additional elements within it, this is represented by a small triangle next to it. Additional information in List view, such as file size and last modified date, is included in columns to the right

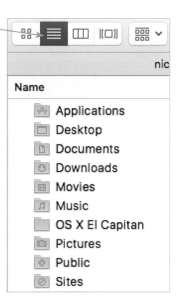

List view can be customized to include a variety of information such as file size and date last modified.

Column view

Column view is a useful option if you want to trace the location of a particular item, i.e. see the full path of its location, starting from the hard drive:

1 Click here on the Finder toolbar to access **Column** view

2 Click on an item to see everything within that folder. If an arrow follows an item it means that there are further items to view

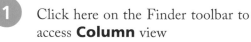

57

Covers

Covers is another innovative feature on the Mac, which enables you to view items as large icons. This is particularly useful for image files as it enables you to quickly see the details of the image to see if it is the one you want. To use Covers:

 Select a folder and at the top of the Finder window click on this button

The items within the folder are displayed in their cover state

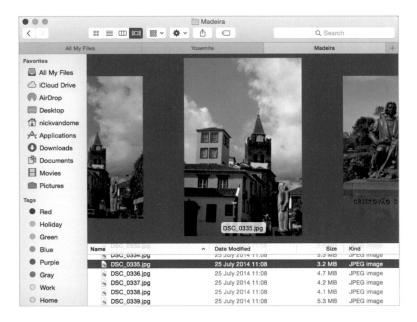

Drag with the mouse on each item to view the next one, or click on the slider at the bottom of the window. You can also move between items by swiping left or right on a trackpad or Magic Mouse

Quick Look

Through a Finder option called Quick Look, it is possible to view the content of a file without having to first open it. To do this:

 Select a file within the Finder

2 Press the space bar

3 The contents of the file are displayed without it opening in its default program

In Quick Look it is even possible to preview videos or presentations without having to first open them in their default program.

4 Click on the cross to close Quick Look

Finder Toolbar

Customizing the toolbar

As with most elements of OS X, it is possible to customize the Finder toolbar. To do this:

1 Select **View > Customize Toolbar...** from the Menu bar

View	Go	Window	Help
as Icons			⌘1
as List			⌘2
✓ as Columns			⌘3
as Cover Flow			⌘4
Clean Up Selection			
Clean Up By			▶
Arrange By			▶
Hide Tab Bar			⇧⌘T
Show Path Bar			⌥⌘P
Show Status Bar			⌘/
Hide Sidebar			⌥⌘S
Hide Preview			⇧⌘P
Hide Toolbar			⌥⌘T
Customize Toolbar...			
Show View Options			⌘J
Enter Full Screen			^⌘F

Beware

Do not put too many items on the Finder toolbar, because you may not be able to see them all in the Finder window. If there are additional toolbar items, there will be a directional arrow indicating this. Click on the arrow to view the available items.

2 Drag items from the window into the toolbar, or

Drag your favorite items into the toolbar...

< >	☰	⊞	⊟ ☰ ▦	❚□❙	✿	⏏	☢	☐	←⟷→
Back	Path	Arrange	View		Action	Eject	Burn	Space	Flexible Space

⌸	🗑	🖧	ⓘ	🔍		👁	⬆	⬯
New Folder	Delete	Connect	Get Info	Search		Quick Look	Share	Edit Tags

3 Drag the default set of icons into the toolbar

... or drag the default set into the toolbar.

< >	⊞ ☰ ▦	❚□❙	⊞ ▾	✿ ▾	⬆	⬯	🔍
Back	View		Arrange	Action	Share	Edit Tags	Search

4 Click **Done** at the bottom of the window

Finder Sidebar

Using the sidebar

The sidebar is the left-hand panel of the Finder which can be used to access items on your Mac. To use this:

 Click on a button on the sidebar

 Its contents are displayed in the main Finder window

Adding to the sidebar

Items that you access most frequently can be added to the sidebar. To do this:

1 Drag an item from the main Finder window onto the sidebar

2 The item is added to the sidebar. You can do this with apps, folders and files

Don't forget

When you click on an item in the sidebar, its contents are shown in the main Finder window to the right.

Don't forget

When items are added to the Finder sidebar, a shortcut, or alias, is inserted into the sidebar, not the actual item.

Don't forget

Items can be removed from the sidebar by Ctrl + clicking on them and selecting **Remove from Sidebar** from the contextual menu.

Finder Search

Searching electronic data is now a massive industry, with companies such as Google leading the way with online searching. On Macs it is also possible to search your folders and files, using the built-in search facilities. This can be done either through the Finder or with the Spotlight app (see pages 108-109).

Using Finder

To search for items within the Finder:

Don't forget

Try to make your search keywords and phrases as accurate as possible. This will create a better list of search results.

1 In the Finder window, enter the search keyword(s) in this box. Search options are listed below the keyword

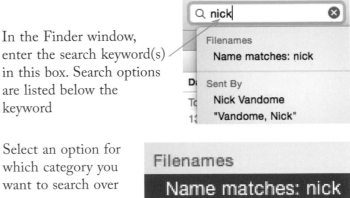

2 Select an option for which category you want to search over

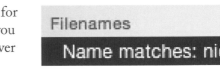

3 The Search results are shown in the Finder window. Click on one of these buttons to search specific areas

Don't forget

Both folders and files will be displayed in the Finder as part of the search results.

4 Double-click on a file to open it

Copying and Moving Items

Items can be copied and moved within OS X by using the copy and paste method or by dragging.

Copy and paste

1 Select an item and select **Edit > Copy** from the Menu bar

2 Move to the target location and select **Edit > Paste Item** from the Menu bar. The item is then pasted into the new location

When an item is copied, it is placed on the Clipboard and remains there until another item is copied.

Dragging

Drag a file from one location to another to move it to that location.

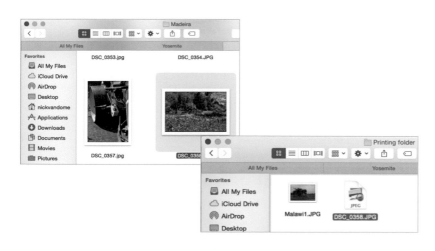

Working with Folders

When OS X El Capitan is installed, there are various folders that have already been created to hold apps and files. Some of these are essential (i.e. those containing apps), while others are created as an aid for where you might want to store the files that you create (such as the Pictures and Movies folders). Once you start working with OS X El Capitan you will probably want to create your own folders in which to store and organize your documents. This can be done on the Desktop or within any level of your existing folder structure. To create a new folder:

Folders are always denoted by a folder icon. This is the same regardless of the Finder view which is selected. The only difference is that the icon is larger in Icon view than in List or Column views.

You can create as many "nested" folders, i.e. folders within other folders, as you want. However, this makes your folder structure more complicated and, after time, you may forget where all your folders are and what they contain.

1 Access the location in which you want to create the new folder (e.g. your Home folder) and select **File > New Folder** from the Menu bar

2 A new, empty folder is inserted at the selected location (named "untitled folder")

3 Overtype the file name with a new one. Press **Enter**

4 Double-click on a folder to view its contents (at this point it should be empty)

Content can be added to an empty folder by dragging it from another folder and dropping it into the new one.

Selecting Items

Apps and files within OS X folders can be selected by a variety of different methods.

Selecting by dragging

Drag the cursor to encompass the items to be selected. The selected items will become highlighted.

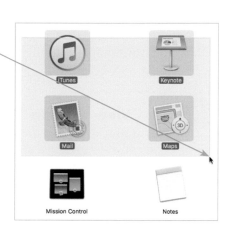

Once items have been selected, a single command can be applied to all of them. For instance, you can copy a group of items by selecting them and then applying the **Copy** command from the Menu bar.

Selecting by clicking

Click once on an item to select it, hold down Shift and then click on another item in a list to select a consecutive group of items.

To select all of the items in a folder, select **Edit > Select All** from the Menu bar. The Select All command selects all of the elements within the active item. For instance, if the active item is a word processing document, the Select All command will select all of the items within the document; if it is a folder, it will select all of the items within that folder.

To select a non-consecutive group, select the first item by clicking on it once, then hold down the Command key (⌘) and select the other required items. The selected items will appear highlighted.

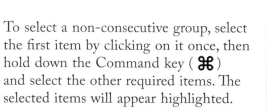

Finder Tabs

Tabs in web browsers are now well established, where you can have several pages open within the same browser window. This technology is included in the Finder in OS X El Capitan with Finder Tabs. This enables different folders to be open in different tabs within the Finder so that you can organize your content exactly how you want. To do this:

 Select **View > Show Tab Bar** from the Finder menu

 A new tab is opened at the right-hand side of the Finder

 Click on this button to view the new tab

4 At this point the content in the new tab is displayed for the window (see tip)

Don't forget

To specify an option for what appears as the default window for a new Finder window tab, click on the **Finder** menu and click on **Preferences** and the **General** tab. Under **New Finder windows show**, select the default window to be used.

5 Access a new folder to display this as the content for the tab. In this way you can use different tabs for different types of content, such as photos or music, or for different topics such as Work, Travel or Finance within Documents

Dozens of tabs can be added in the Finder. However, when there are too many to fit along the Tab Bar they are stacked on top of each other, so it can be hard to work out what you have in your tabs.

6 Each tab view can be customized and this is independent of the other tabs

Tagging in the Finder

When creating content in OS X El Capitan you may find that you have documents of different types that cover the same topic. For instance, you may have work-related documents in Pages for reports, Keynote for presentations and Numbers for spreadsheets. With the Finder Tags function it is possible to link items with related content through the use of colored tags. These can be added to items in the Finder and also in apps when content is created.

Hot tip

Tags can also be added to items by Ctrl + clicking on them and selecting the required tag from the menu that appears. Also, they can be added from this button on the main Finder toolbar.

1 The tags are listed in the Finder sidebar

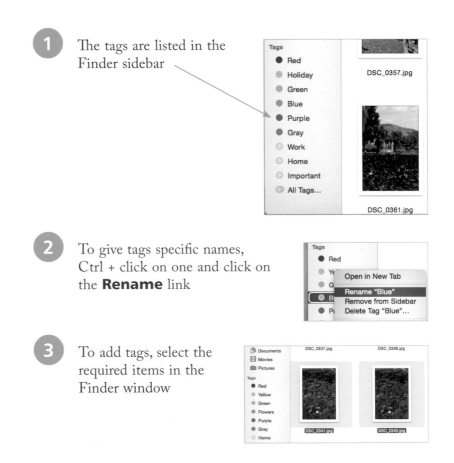

2 To give tags specific names, Ctrl + click on one and click on the **Rename** link

3 To add tags, select the required items in the Finder window

4 Drag the selected items over the appropriate tag

Hot tip

Tags can be dragged onto the Dock so that all items with a specific tag can be accessed from here. To do this, drag the tag from the Finder window to the right-hand side of the Dock's dividing line. This will create a Stack containing all of the items with the selected tag.

The tags are added to the selected items

Adding tags in apps

Tags can also be added when documents are created in certain apps, such as Pages, Keynote and Numbers.

 Select **File > Save**, click in the **Tags** box and select the required tag. Click on the **Save** button

Hot tip

Tags can also be added to iCloud documents so that when you are viewing content in iCloud, all tagged items can be viewed together.

Viewing tags

To view all documents that have had the same tag added:

① Click on the required tag in the Finder sidebar. All of the tagged documents will be displayed, regardless of their content type, or where they are saved on your Mac

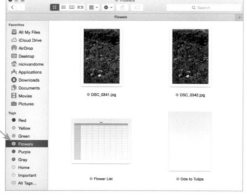

Spring-loaded Folders

Another method for moving items with the Finder is to use the spring-loaded folder option. This enables you to drag items into a folder and then view the contents of the folder before you drop the item into it. This means that you can drag items into nested folders in a single operation. To do this:

Hot tip

The spring-loaded folder technique can be used to move items between different locations within the Finder, e.g. for moving files from your Pictures folder into your Home folder.

1 Select the item you want to move

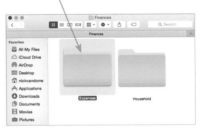

2 Drag the selected item over the folder into which you want to place it. Keep the mouse held down

Beware

Do not release the mouse button until you have reached the location into which you want to place the selected item.

3 The folder will open, revealing its contents. The selected item can either be dropped into the folder or, if there are sub-folders, the same operation can be repeated until you find the folder into which you want to place the selected item. Release the item to complete the operation

Burnable Folders

With the increasing use of images, digital video and music files, computer users are frequently copying data from their computers onto CDs. In some cases this can be a frustrating process but in OS X El Capitan, the use of burnable folders can make the process much quicker. These are folders that can be created specifically for the contents to be burned onto a CD or DVD. To do this:

 In the Finder, select **File > New Burn Folder** from the Menu bar

Burn Folder

71

Hot tip

Applications such as iTunes can be used to burn CDs using the content within that application, but burnable folders are the best way to combine files from a variety of different applications and then burn them onto discs.

2 The burn folder is created in the Finder window which was active when Step 1 was performed. Click on the folder name and overtype to give it a unique name

3 Select the items that you want to burn, and drag and drop or copy and paste them into the burn folder

4 Click on this button to burn the disc **Burn**

Actions Button

The Finder Actions button provides a variety of options for any item, or items, selected in the Finder. To use this:

 1 Select an item, or group of items, about which you want to find out additional information

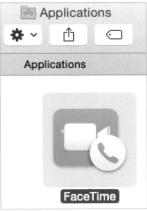

Hot tip

If an image has been selected, the Actions button can be used to set it as the desktop picture, by selecting this option at the bottom of the Actions menu.

2 Click on the **Actions** button on the Finder toolbar

3 The available options for the selected item, or items, are displayed. These include **Get Summary Info** which displays additional information about an item, such as file type, file size, creation and modification dates and the default program for opening the item(s)

New Folder
Open
Show Package Contents

Move to Trash

Get Summary Info
Compress "FaceTime"
Burn "FaceTime" to Disc...
Duplicate
Make Alias
Quick Look "FaceTime"

Copy "FaceTime"

Arrange By ▶
Show View Options

● ● ● ● ○ ● ●

Reveal in Finder

Don't forget

The Actions button can also be used for labeling items with Finder Tags. To do this, select the required items in the Finder and click on the colored tags at the bottom of the Actions button menu. The selected tag will be applied to the item names in the Finder.

Sharing from the Finder

Next to the Actions button on the Finder is the Share button. This can be used to share a selected item, or items, in a variety of ways appropriate to the type of file that has been selected. For instance, a photo will have options including the photo sharing site Flickr, while a text document will have fewer options. To share items directly from the Finder:

1 Locate and select the item(s) that you want to share

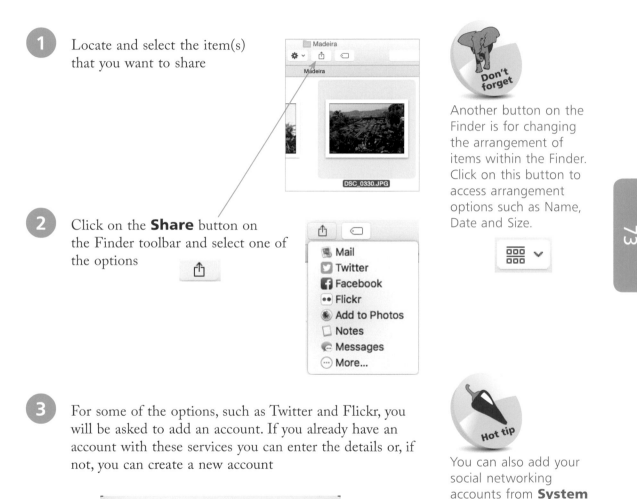

DSC_0330.JPG

2 Click on the **Share** button on the Finder toolbar and select one of the options

- Mail
- Twitter
- Facebook
- Flickr
- Add to Photos
- Notes
- Messages
- More...

3 For some of the options, such as Twitter and Flickr, you will be asked to add an account. If you already have an account with these services you can enter the details or, if not, you can create a new account

flickr

No account is configured

Cancel   Add Account...

Don't forget

Another button on the Finder is for changing the arrangement of items within the Finder. Click on this button to access arrangement options such as Name, Date and Size.

Hot tip

You can also add your social networking accounts from **System Preferences > Internet Accounts**. Select the required account and enter your log in details.

Menus

The main Apple menu bar in OS X El Capitan contains a variety of menus, which are accessed when the Finder is the active window. When individual apps are open they have their own menu bars, although in a lot of cases these are similar to the standard menu bar, particularly for the built-in OS X El Capitan apps such as the Calendar, Contacts and Notes.

- **Apple menu**. This is denoted by a translucent blue apple and contains general information about the computer, a link to the System Preferences, and the App Store for app updates, and options for closing down your Mac.

- **Finder menu**. This contains preference options for amending the functionality and appearance of the Finder and also options for emptying the Trash and accessing other apps (under the Services option).

- **File menu**. This contains common commands for working with open documents, such as opening and closing files, creating aliases, moving to the Trash, ejecting external devices and burning discs.

- **Edit menu**. This contains common commands that apply to the majority of apps used on the Mac. These include undo, cut, copy, paste, select all and show the contents of the clipboard, i.e. items that have been cut or copied.

- **View**. This contains options for how windows and folders are displayed within the Finder and for customizing the Finder toolbar. This includes showing or hiding the Finder sidebar and selecting view options for the size at which icons are displayed within Finder windows.

- **Go**. This can be used to navigate around your computer. This includes moving to your All My Files folder, your Home folder, your Applications folder and recently accessed folders.

- **Window**. This contains commands to organize the currently open apps and files on your desktop.

- **Help**. This contains the Mac Help files which contain information about all aspects of OS X El Capitan.

4   Navigating in OS X El Capitan

OS X El Capitan has Multi–Touch gestures for navigating around your apps and documents. This chapter looks at how to use these to get around your Mac and also using Mission Control.

The OS X Way of Navigating

One of the most revolutionary features of OS X Mountain Lion, Mavericks and Yosemite, which is continued with OS X El Capitan, is the way in which you can navigate around your applications, web pages and documents. This involves a much greater reliance on swiping on a trackpad or adapted mouse; techniques that have been imported from the iPhone and the iPad. These are known as Multi-Touch Gestures and to take full advantage of these you will need to have one of the following devices:

- **A trackpad**. This will be found on MacBooks.

- **A Magic Trackpad**. This can be used with an iMac, a Mac Mini or a Mac Pro. It works wirelessly via Bluetooth.

- **A Magic Mouse**. This can be used with an iMac, a Mac Mini or a Mac Pro. It works wirelessly via Bluetooth.

All of these devices work using a swiping technique with fingers moving over their surface. This should be done with a light touch; it is a gentle swipe, rather than any pressure being applied to the device.

The trackpads and Magic Mouse do not have any buttons in the same way as traditional devices. Instead, specific areas are clickable so that you can still perform left- and right-click operations.

On a Magic Mouse the center and right side can be used for clicking operations and on a Magic Trackpad the left and right corners can perform the same tasks.

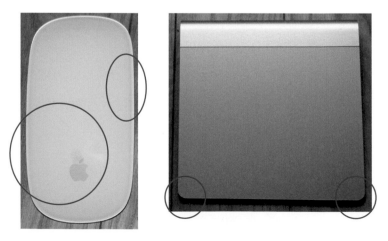

Hot tip

The latest models of MacBooks, released in May 2015, (and the Magic Trackpad 2) employ a technology known as Force Touch. This provides the user with different options, depending on how firmly they press on the trackpad. This means that more than one function can be performed, simply by pressing more firmly on the trackpad. It also provides haptic feedback, which is a physical response from the trackpad in the form of a small vibration, once different options have been accessed.

OS X Scroll Bars

In OS X El Capitan, scroll bars in web pages and documents are more reactive to the navigational device being used on the computer. By default, with a Magic Trackpad, a trackpad or a Magic Mouse scroll bars are only visible when scrolling is actually taking place. However, if a mouse is being used they will be visible permanently, although this can be changed for all devices. To perform scrolling with OS X El Capitan:

1 Scroll around a web page or document by swiping up or down on a Magic Mouse, a Magic Trackpad, or a trackpad. As you move up or down the scroll bar appears

If you do not have a trackpad, a Magic Trackpad or a Magic Mouse you can still navigate in OS X El Capitan with a traditional mouse and the use of scroll bars in windows.

2 When you stop scrolling the bar disappears, to allow optimum viewing area for your web page or document

3 To change the scroll bar options, select **System Preferences > General** and select the required settings under **Show scroll bars**

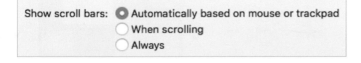

Show scroll bars: ● Automatically based on mouse or trackpad
○ When scrolling
○ Always

Split View

When working with computers it can sometimes be beneficial to be able to view two windows next to each other. This can be to compare information in two different windows, or just to be able to use two windows without having to access them from the Desktop each time. In OS X El Capitan, two windows can be displayed next to each other using the Split View feature:

1 By default, all open windows are layered on top of each other, with the active one at the top

If you click once on the green maximize button this will display the app in full screen mode, rather than holding on it to activate Split View.

2 Press and hold on the green maximize button to activate Split View. The active window is displayed on the left-hand side of the screen, with thumbnails of the other open apps on the right-hand side

3 Click on one of the apps on the right-hand side in Step 2 to add it as the other Split View panel. Click on each window in Split View to make it active

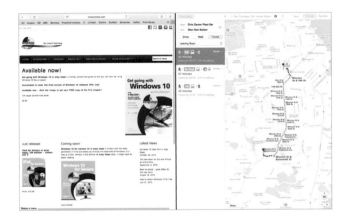

You can work on one panel in Split View, i.e. move through web pages, without affecting the content of the app on the other side.

4 Drag the middle divider bar to resize either of the Split View panels, to change the viewing area

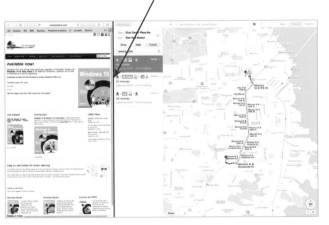

Swap the windows in Split View by dragging the top toolbar of one app into the other window.

5 Move the cursor over the left-hand edge of the window to display the sidebar menu for that app, if it has one

Trackpad Gestures

Pointing and clicking

A Magic Trackpad, or trackpad, can be used to perform a variety of pointing and clicking tasks:

Don't forget

By default, the iMac with Retina Display, comes with a Magic Mouse provided. However, this can be swapped for a Magic Trackpad, or both can be included for an additional price.

1 Tap with one finger in the middle of the Magic Trackpad, or trackpad, to perform a single click operation, e.g. to click on a button or click on an open window

2 Tap once with two fingers in the middle of the Magic Trackpad, or trackpad, to access any contextual menus associated with an item (this is the equivalent of the traditional right-click with a mouse)

3 Highlight a word or phrase and double-tap with three fingers to see look-up information for the selected item. This is frequently a dictionary definition but it can also be a Wikipedia entry

4 Move over an item and drag with three fingers to move the item around the screen

Beware

If you have too many functions set using the same number of fingers, some of them may not work. See pages 91-92 for details about setting preferences for Multi-Touch Gestures.

...cont'd

Scrolling and zooming

One of the most common operations on a computer is scrolling on a page, whether it is a web page or a document. Traditionally, this has been done with a mouse and a cursor. However, using a Magic Trackpad you can now do all of your scrolling with your fingers. There are a number of options for doing this.

Scrolling up and down

To move up and down web pages or documents, use two fingers on the Magic Trackpad, or trackpad, and swipe up or down. The page moves in the opposite direction to the one in which you are swiping, i.e. if you swipe up, the page moves down and vice versa.

Don't worry if you cannot immediately get the hang of Multi-Touch Gestures. It takes a bit of practice to get the correct touch and pressure on the Magic Trackpad, a trackpad or the Magic Mouse.

 Open a web page

 Position two fingers in the middle of the Magic Trackpad, or trackpad

3 Swipe them up to move down the page

When scrolling up and down pages, the gesture moves the page the opposite way, i.e. swipe down to move up the page and vice versa.

4 Swipe them down to move up a page

...cont'd

Zooming in and out

To zoom in or out on web pages or documents:

 To zoom in, position your thumb and forefinger in the middle of the Magic Trackpad, or trackpad

Pages can also be zoomed in on by double-tapping with two fingers.

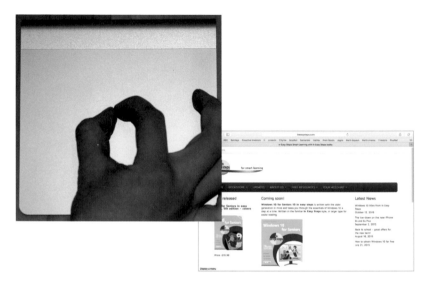

 Spread them outwards to zoom in on a web page or document

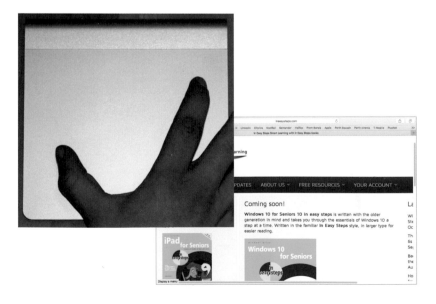

...cont'd

3 To zoom out, position your thumb and forefinger at opposite corners of the Magic Trackpad, or trackpad

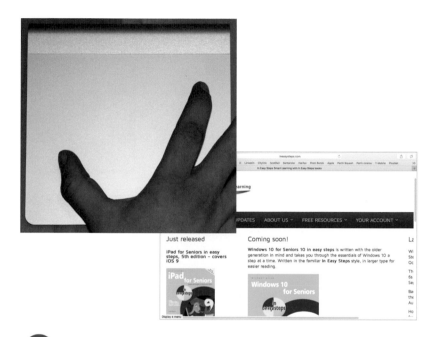

There is a limit on how far you can zoom in or out on a web page or document, to ensure that it does not distort the content too much.

4 Pinch them into the center of the Magic Trackpad, or trackpad, to zoom out

...cont'd

Moving between pages

With Multi-Touch Gestures, it is possible to swipe between pages within a document. To do this:

 Position two fingers to the left or right of the Magic Trackpad, or trackpad

 Swipe to the opposite side of the Magic Trackpad, or trackpad, to move through the document

See pages 98-99 for details about using full screen apps.

Moving between full screen apps

In addition to moving between pages by swiping, it is also possible to move between different apps when they are in full screen mode. To do this:

 Position three fingers to the left or right of the Magic Trackpad, or trackpad

 Swipe to the opposite side of the Magic Trackpad, or trackpad, to move through the available full screen apps

Showing the Desktop

To show the whole Desktop, regardless of how many files or apps are open:

 Position your thumb and three fingers in the middle of the Magic Trackpad, or trackpad

2 Swipe to the opposite corners of the Magic Trackpad, or trackpad, to display the Desktop

3 The Desktop is displayed, with all items minimized around the side of the screen

Magic Mouse Gestures

Pointing and clicking

A Magic Mouse can be used to perform a variety of pointing and clicking tasks:

 Click with one finger on the Magic Mouse to perform a single-click operation, e.g. to select a button or command

The right-click operation can be set within the Mouse System Preferences.

2 Tap with one finger on the right side of the Magic Mouse to access any contextual menus associated with an item (this is the equivalent of the traditional right-click with a mouse)

...cont'd

Scrolling and zooming
The Magic Mouse can also be used to perform scrolling and zooming functions within a web page or document:

 Swipe up or down with one finger to move up or down a web page or document

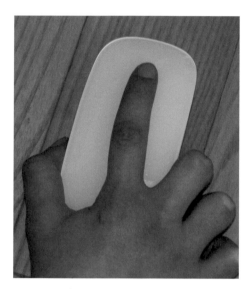

Don't forget

When scrolling on a web page or document, it moves in the opposite direction to the movement of your finger, i.e. if you swipe up, the page moves down and vice versa.

Double-tap with one finger to zoom in on a web page

...cont'd

3 Swipe left or right with one finger to move between pages

4 Swipe left or right with two fingers to move between full screen apps

Multi-Touch Preferences

Some Multi-Touch Gestures only have a single action, which cannot be changed. However, others have options for changing the action for a specific gesture. This is done within the respective preferences for the Magic Mouse, the Magic Trackpad or the trackpad, where a full list of Multi-Touch Gestures is shown. To use these:

1 Access the System Preferences and click on the **Mouse** or **Trackpad** button

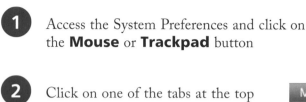

2 Click on one of the tabs at the top

3 The actions are described on the left, with a graphic explanation on the right

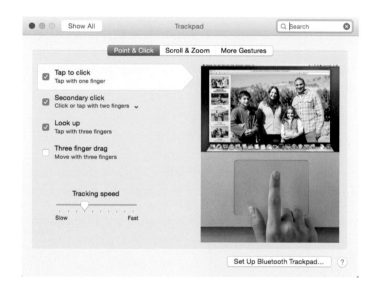

91

The Magic Trackpad, or trackpad, has three tabbed options within the System Preferences: Point & Click, Scroll & Zoom and More Gestures. The Magic Mouse has preferences for Point & Click and More Gestures.

4 If there is a down arrow next to an option, click on it to change the way an action is activated

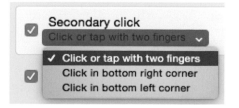

...cont'd

Trackpad Gestures
The full list of trackpad Multi-Touch Gestures, with their default action are (relevant ones for Magic Mouse are in brackets):

Point & Click

- Tap to click – tap once with one finger (same for the Magic Mouse)

- Secondary click – click or tap with two fingers (single-click on the right of the Magic Mouse)

- Look up – double-tap with three fingers

- Three finger drag – move with three fingers

Scroll & Zoom

- Scroll direction: natural – content tracks finger movement, with two fingers (one finger with the Magic Mouse)

- Zoom in or out – spread or pinch with two fingers

- Smart zoom – double-tap with two fingers (double-tap with one finger with the Magic Mouse)

- Rotate – rotate with two fingers

More Gestures

- Swipe between pages – scroll left or right with two fingers (scroll left or right with one finger with the Magic Mouse)

- Swipe between full screen apps – swipe left or right with three fingers (swipe left or right with two fingers with the Magic Mouse)

- Swipe left from the right-hand edge of the trackpad or Magic Trackpad to access the Notification Center

- Access Mission Control (see next page) – swipe up with three fingers (double-tap with two fingers with the Magic Mouse)

- App Exposé – swipe down with three fingers

- Access Launchpad – pinch with thumb and three fingers

- Show Desktop – spread with thumb and three fingers

Don't forget

Natural scrolling means the page follows the direction of your finger, vertically or horizontally, depending on which way you're scrolling.

Hot tip

Exposé enables you to view all of the active windows that are currently open for a particular app.

Mission Control

Mission Control is a function in OS X El Capitan that helps you organize all of your open apps, full screen apps and documents. It also enables you to quickly view the Desktop. Within Mission Control there is also Spaces, where you can group together similar types of documents. To use Mission Control:

 1 Click on this button on the Dock, or Swipe upwards with three fingers on the Magic Trackpad or trackpad, or double-tap with two fingers on a Magic Mouse

2 All open files and apps are visible via Mission Control

3 If there is more than one window open for an app they will each be shown separately

4 Move the cursor over the top of the Mission Control window to view the different Spaces (see next page) and any apps in full screen mode

Desktop 1   Photos

Click on a window in Mission Control to access it and exit the Mission Control window.

Any apps or files that have been minimized or closed do not appear within the main Mission Control window. Instead, they are located to the right of the dividing line on the Dock.

Drag an open app to the top of the screen to access Mission Control. You can also make an app full screen from Mission Control by dragging it onto one of the Spaces at the top of the window.

Spaces

The top level of Mission Control contains Spaces, which are areas into which you can group certain apps, e.g. the iWork apps such as Pages and Numbers. This means that you can access these apps independently from every other open item. This helps organize your apps and files. To use Spaces:

Don't forget

Preferences for Spaces can be set within the Mission Control System Preference.

Hot tip

Create different Spaces for different types of content, e.g. one for productivity and one for entertainment.

Don't forget

When you create a new Space it can subsequently be deleted by moving the cursor over it and clicking on the cross at the left-hand corner. Any items that have been added to this Space are returned to the default Desktop Space.

1 Move the cursor over the top right-hand corner of Mission Control and click on the **+** symbol

2 A new **Space** is created along the top row of Mission Control

Desktop 3

3 Drag an app onto the Space

Desktop 3

4 Drag additional apps onto the Space. This can be accessed by clicking on the Space within Mission Control, and all of the apps that have been placed here will be available

Desktop 3

5 OS X El Capitan Apps

Apps are the programs with which you start putting OS X El Capitan to use, either for work or for fun. This chapter looks at using apps and the online App Store.

Launchpad

Even though the Dock can be used to store shortcuts to your applications, it is limited in terms of space. The full set of applications on your Mac can be found in the Finder (see Chapter Three) but OS X El Capitan has a feature that allows you to quickly access and manage all of your applications. These include the ones that are pre-installed on your Mac and also any that you install yourself or download from the Apple App Store. This feature is called Launchpad. To use it:

Hot tip

If the apps take up more than one screen, swipe from right to left with two fingers to view the additional pages, or click on the buttons at the bottom of the window.

1 Click once on this button on the Dock

Don't forget

To launch an app from within Launchpad, click on it once.

2 All of the apps (applications) are displayed

Hot tip

One of the apps in Utilities is Boot Camp Assistant, which can be used to run Windows on your Mac, if required.

3 Similar types of apps can be grouped together in individual folders. By default, the **Utilities** are grouped in this way

4 To create a group of similar apps, drag the icon for one over another

5 The apps are grouped together in a new folder and Launchpad gives it a name, based on the types of apps within the folder, usually the one into which the selected app is placed

6 To change the name, click on it once and overtype it with the new name

7 The folder appears within the **Launchpad** window

8 To remove an app, click and hold on it until it starts to jiggle and a cross appears. Click on the cross to remove it

System apps, i.e. the ones that already come with your Mac, cannot be removed from the Launchpad, only ones you have downloaded.

Full Screen Apps

When working with apps, we all like to be able to see as much of a window as possible. With OS X El Capitan this is possible with the full screen app option. This functionality allows you to expand an app so that it takes up the whole of your monitor or screen with a minimum of toolbars visible. Some apps have this functionality but some do not. To use full screen apps:

1 By default, an app appears on the Desktop with other windows behind it

If the button in Step 2 is not visible then the app does not have the full screen functionality.

2 Click on this button at the top left-hand corner of the app's window

3 The app is expanded to take up the whole window. The main Apple Menu bar and the Dock are hidden

...cont'd

4 To view the
main Menu bar,
move the cursor over the top of the screen

5 You can move between all full screen apps by swiping
with three fingers left or right on a trackpad or Magic
Mouse

For more information
about navigating with
Multi-Touch Gestures see
pages 80-90.

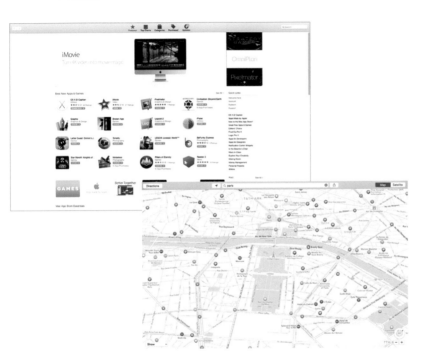

6 Move the cursor over the top left-hand corner of
the screen and click on this button to close the
full screen functionality

7 In Mission Control all of the open full screen apps are
shown in the top row

The OS X apps can be accessed from the Launchpad and also from the Applications folder within the Finder.

There are not many games apps with OS X, but one of them is the Chess app.

Hot tip

For qualifying Macs with OS X El Capitan, the iWork apps (Pages, Numbers and Keynote) are free to download from the App Store, or come pre-installed.

Don't forget

Several apps are available in the App Store for watching YouTube videos. This can also be done from the YouTube website using Safari.

OS X Apps

OS X El Capitan apps include:

- **Automator**. An app for creating automated processes

- **Calculator**. A basic calculator

- **Calendar**. (See pages 112-113)

- **Contacts**. (See pages 110-111)

- **Dashboard**. A range of widgets to use on your Mac

- **Dictionary**. A digital dictionary

- **DVD Player**. Used to play and view DVDs

- **FaceTime**. Used for video calls (See page 144)

- **Font Book**. Use this to add and change fonts

- **Game Center**. The app for playing games on your Mac

- **iBooks**. An app for downloading ebooks (See pages 154-155)

- **iTunes, Photos, iMovie, and GarageBand.** (See Chapter Eight. The Photos app supersedes iPhoto)

- **Mail**. The default email app

- **Maps**. For viewing locations and destinations worldwide

- **Messages**. (See pages 142-143)

- **Mission Control**. The function for organizing your Desktop

- **Notes**. (See pages 114-115)

- **Photo Booth**. An app for creating photo effects

- **Preview**. (See page 124)

- **QuickTime Player**. Apple's own app for viewing video

- **Reminders**. (See pages 116-117)

- **Safari**. The OS X specific web browser

- **TextEdit**. An app for editing text files

- **Time Machine**. OS X's backup facility

Accessing the App Store

The App Store is another OS X app. This is an online facility where you can download and buy new apps. These cover a range of categories such as productivity, business and entertainment. When you select or buy an app from the App Store, it is downloaded automatically to Launchpad and appears there next to the rest of the apps.

To buy apps from the App Store you need to have an Apple ID. If you have not already set this up, it can be done when you first access the App Store. To use the App Store:

Don't forget

The App Store is an online function so you will need an internet connection with which to access it.

1 Click on this icon on the Dock or within the Launchpad

2 The Homepage of the App Store contains the current top featured and best new apps

Hot tip

You can set up an Apple ID when you first set up your Mac or you can do it when you register for the App Store or the iTunes Store.

3 Your account information and quick link categories are listed at the right-hand side of the page

Quick Links

Welcome Nick
Account
Redeem
Support

OS X El Capitan
Apps Made by Apple
New to the Mac App Store?
Great Free Apps & Games
Editors' Choice

Downloading Apps

The App Store contains a wide range of apps: from small, fun apps, to powerful productivity ones. However, downloading them from the App Store is the same regardless of the type of app. The only differences are whether they need to be paid for or not and the length of time they take to download. To download an app from the App Store:

 Browse through the App Store until you find the required app

 Click on the app to view a detailed description about it

 Click on the button underneath the app icon to download it. If there is no charge for the app the button will say **Get**

Hot tip

When downloading apps, start with a free one first so that you can get used to the process before you download paid-for apps.

4 If there is a charge for the app, the
button will say **Buy App**

5 Click on the **Install App** button

6 Enter your **Apple ID** account details to continue
downloading the app

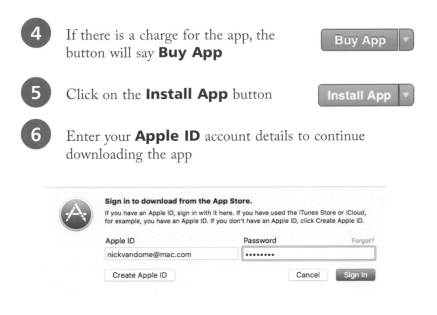

Sign in to download from the App Store.
If you have an Apple ID, sign in with it here. If you have used the iTunes Store or iCloud,
for example, you have an Apple ID. If you don't have an Apple ID, click Create Apple ID.

Apple ID	Password	Forgot?
nickvandome@mac.com	••••••••	

Create Apple ID   Cancel   Sign In

Depending on their
size, different apps take
differing amounts of
time to be downloaded.

7 The progress of the download is displayed
in a progress bar underneath the
Launchpad icon on the Dock

8 Once it has been downloaded, the app
is available within Launchpad

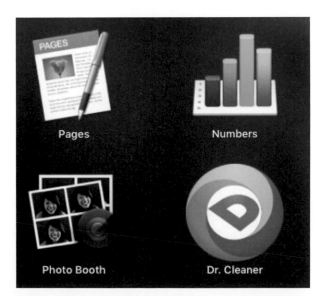

Pages   Numbers

Photo Booth   Dr. Cleaner

As you download more
apps, additional pages
will be created within
the Launchpad to
accommodate them.

Finding Apps

There are thousands of apps in the App Store and sometimes the hardest task is locating the ones you want. However, there are a number of ways in which finding apps is made as easy as possible:

 Click on the **Featured** button

 The main window has a range of categories such as New & Noteworthy and What's Hot. At the right-hand side there is a panel with the **Top Paid** apps

Hot tip

Another way to find apps is to type a keyword into the Search box at the top right-hand corner of the App Store window.

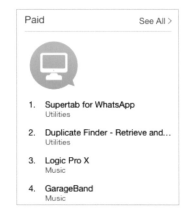

Paid   See All >

1. Supertab for WhatsApp
   Utilities
2. Duplicate Finder - Retrieve and...
   Utilities
3. Logic Pro X
   Music
4. GarageBand
   Music

 Underneath this is a list of the **Top Free** apps

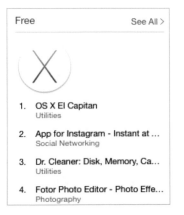

Free   See All >

1. OS X El Capitan
   Utilities
2. App for Instagram - Instant at ...
   Social Networking
3. Dr. Cleaner: Disk, Memory, Ca...
   Utilities
4. Fotor Photo Editor - Photo Effe...
   Photography

Click on the **Top Charts** button

 The top apps for different categories are displayed

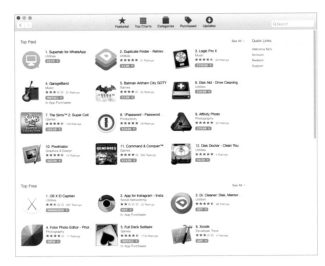

 Click on the **Categories** button

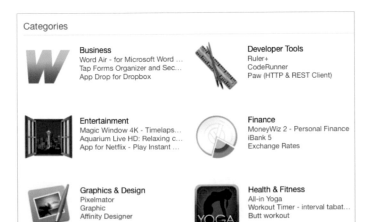

Browse through the apps by specific categories, such as Business, Entertainment and Finance

The Top Charts has sections for paid-for apps and free ones. There is also a sidebar for Top Charts Categories to view the top items in each category.

105

Even if you interrupt a download and turn off your Mac you will still be able to resume the download when you restart your computer.

If a download of an app has been interrupted, click on the **Resume** button to continue downloading it.

Apps can also be updated automatically. This can be specified in **System Preferences > App Store**. Check **On** the **Automatically check for updates** option. Underneath this there are options for downloading and installing updates.

Managing Your Apps

Once you have bought apps from the App Store you can view details of the ones you have purchased and also install updated versions of them.

Purchased Apps
To view your purchased apps:

1 Click on the **Purchased** button

2 Details of your purchased apps are displayed (including those that are free)

Updating Apps
Improvements and fixes are being developed constantly and these can be downloaded to ensure that all of your apps are up-to-date:

1 When updates are available this is indicated by a red circle on the App Store icon in the Dock or Launchpad, in the same way as you would be alerted to new emails

2 Click on the **Updates** button

3 Information about the update is displayed next to the app that is due to be updated

4 Click on the **Update** button to update an individual app

5 Click on the **Update All** button to update all of the apps that are due to be updated

6 Getting Productive

There are several built-in apps within OS X El Capitan that can be used to create, store and display information. This chapter shows how to access and use these apps, so that you can get the most out of OS X El Capitan as a productive and smooth-running tool.

Spotlight Search

Spotlight is the dedicated search app for OS X. It can be used over all the files on your Mac and the internet. To use Spotlight:

 Click on this icon at the far right of the Apple Menu bar

 The Spotlight Search can show results from your Mac, the internet, iTunes, the App Store and also items such as movies nearby and local restaurants

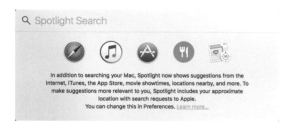

 Click in the Spotlight Search box

 Enter a keyword, or phrase, for which you want to search

 The top hits from within your apps are shown in the left-hand panel. Click on one to view its details

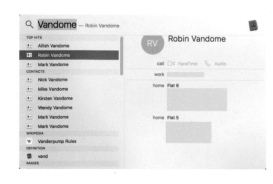

The Spotlight Search window can also be resized and dragged into any position on the screen.

6 Scroll down the left-hand panel to view different search result options, such as entries from Wikipedia, or a dictionary definition of a word

Hot tip

Since the Spotlight Search is always visible, it can be a quicker way to look for items than the Finder search function.

7 There are also website suggestions based on the search terms and you can also select to search over the web

Beware

Spotlight starts searching for items as soon as you start typing a word. So don't worry if some of the first results look inappropriate, as these will disappear once you have finished typing the full word.

8 Click and hold on the top of the Spotlight Search window to drag it into a new position on the screen

Contacts (Address Book)

The Contacts app can be used to store contact information, which can then be used in different apps and shared via iCloud. To view and add contacts:

1 Open your **Contacts** and click on one in the left-hand panel to view their details

Adding contact information

The main function of the Contacts app is to include details of personal and business contacts. This has to be done manually for each entry, but it can prove to be a valuable resource once it has been completed. To add contact information:

1 Click on the **Edit** button to edit contacts   Edit

2 Click on a category and enter contact information. Press the **Tab** key to move to the next field

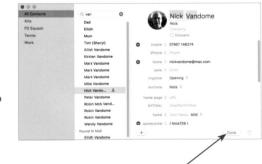

3 Click on the **Done** button once you have edited the entry

Creating groups

In addition to creating individual entries in the Contacts app, group contacts can also be created. This is a way of grouping contacts with similar interests. Once a group has been created, all of the entries within it can be accessed and contacted by selecting the relevant entry in the left-hand panel. To create a group:

1 Select **File > New Group** from the Menu bar to create a new group entry

2 Give the new group a name

3 Drag individual entries into the group (the individual entries are retained too)

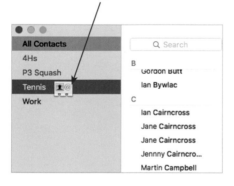

4 Click on a group name to view the members of the group

Individuals can be included in several groups. If you change their details in one group, these changes will take effect across all of the groups in which the entry occurs.

Groups in your contacts can be used to send group emails, i.e. you can type the name of the group into the **Mail To** box to generate the names in the group and send the email to all of these recipients.

111

Calendar

Electronic calendars are now a standard part of modern life and with OS X this function is performed by the Calendar app. Not only can this be used on your Mac, it can also be synchronized with other Apple devices such as an iPod or an iPhone, using iCloud. To create a calendar:

Hot tip

When Calendar is opened it displays the current date in the icon on the Dock.

 1 Click on this icon on the Dock, or in the Launchpad

 2 Select whether to view the calendar by day, week, month or year

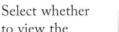

 3 In month view, the current day is denoted by a red circle on the date

Don't forget

Click on the **Today** button to view the current day. Click on the forward or back arrows to move to the next day, week, month or year, depending on what is selected in Step 2.

112

Hot tip

If Family Sharing has been activated, the Family calendar will automatically be added, for all members of the Family Sharing group.

 4 Scroll up and down to move through the weeks and months. In OS X El Capitan this is done with continuous scrolling which means you can view weeks across different months, rather than just viewing each month in its entirety, i.e. you can view the second half of one month and the first half of the next one in the same window

Adding Events

 Select a date and double-click on it, or Ctrl + click on the date. Select **New Event**

 Click on the **New Event** field and enter an event name

3 Click on the date or time to amend it by entering new details. Check on the all-day box to set the event for a whole day

Finding Locations

When adding events you can also find details about locations:

1 Click on the **Add Location** field and start typing a destination. Suggestions will appear underneath, including matching items from your contacts list. Click on a location to select it

2 A map of the location is displayed, including a real-time weather summary for the location. Click on the map to view it in greater detail in the **Maps** app

Taking Notes

It is always useful to have a quick way of making notes of everyday things, such as shopping lists, recipes or packing lists for traveling. With OS X El Capitan, the Notes app is perfect for this task. To use it:

Don't forget

Enable iCloud for Notes so that all of your notes will be backed up and also available on all of your iCloud-enabled devices. You will also be able to access them by signing in to your account with your Apple ID at www.icloud.com

Don't forget

The first line of a note becomes its heading in the notes panel.

Hot tip

Click on this button to view the Attachments Browser to view all of the items you have added to your notes. You can then select an item for a new note.

1 Click on this icon on the Dock, or in the Launchpad

2 The right-hand panel is where the note is created. The middle panel displays a list of all notes

3 Click on this button to add a new note

4 As more notes are added, the most recent appears at the top of the list in the middle panel

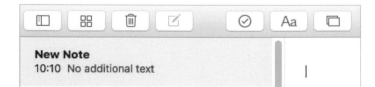

5 Click on this button to show or hide the left-hand panel in the Notes app, which displays the notes folders

Formatting notes

In OS X El Capitan there are a number of new formatting options for the Notes app:

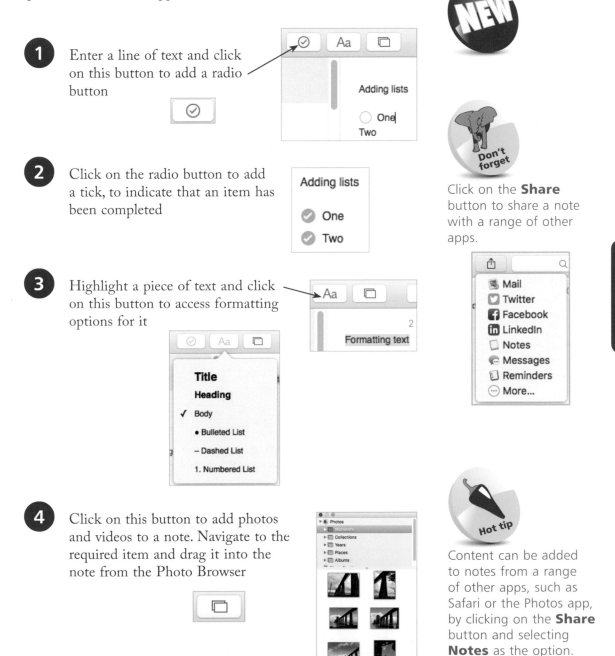

1 Enter a line of text and click on this button to add a radio button

2 Click on the radio button to add a tick, to indicate that an item has been completed

3 Highlight a piece of text and click on this button to access formatting options for it

4 Click on this button to add photos and videos to a note. Navigate to the required item and drag it into the note from the Photo Browser

NEW

Don't forget

Click on the **Share** button to share a note with a range of other apps.

Hot tip

Content can be added to notes from a range of other apps, such as Safari or the Photos app, by clicking on the **Share** button and selecting **Notes** as the option.

Setting Reminders

Another useful app for keeping organized is Reminders. This enables you to create lists for different topics and then set reminders for specific items. A date and time can be set for each reminder and, when this is reached, the reminder appears on your Mac screen (and in the Notification Center). To use Reminders:

Don't forget

As with Notes, iCloud makes your reminders available on all of your Apple devices, i.e. your Mac, iPad, iPhone and iPod Touch.

 Click on this icon on the Dock, or in the Launchpad

 Lists can be created for different categories of reminders. The Reminder lists are located in the left-hand panel. Click on a list name to add lists here

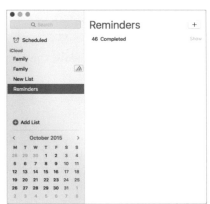

 Click on this button to add a new reminder, or click on a new line

4 Enter text for the reminder

5 Click on this button to add details for the reminder

Hot tip

Roll over a reminder name to access the 'i' symbol for adding details to the reminder.

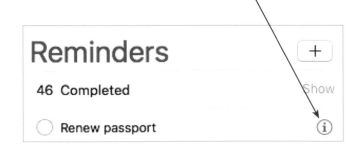

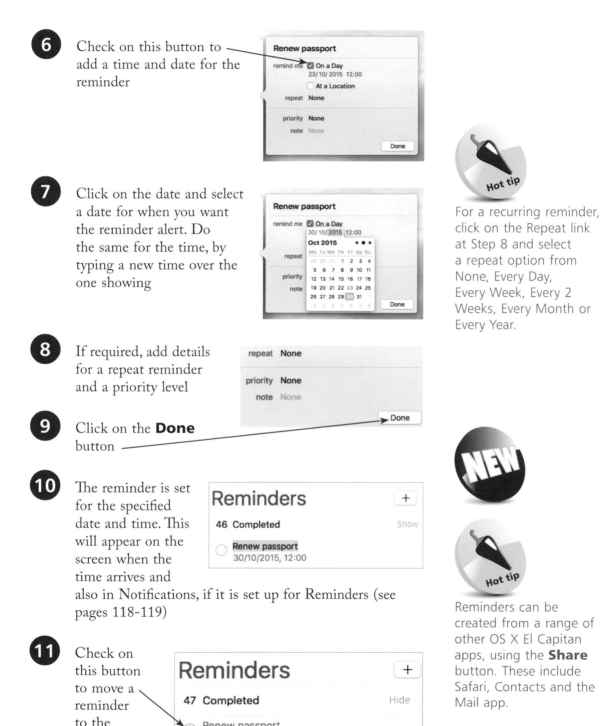

6 Check on this button to add a time and date for the reminder

7 Click on the date and select a date for when you want the reminder alert. Do the same for the time, by typing a new time over the one showing

8 If required, add details for a repeat reminder and a priority level

9 Click on the **Done** button

10 The reminder is set for the specified date and time. This will appear on the screen when the time arrives and also in Notifications, if it is set up for Reminders (see pages 118-119)

11 Check on this button to move a reminder to the Completed list

Hot tip

For a recurring reminder, click on the Repeat link at Step 8 and select a repeat option from None, Every Day, Every Week, Every 2 Weeks, Every Month or Every Year.

117

Hot tip

Reminders can be created from a range of other OS X El Capitan apps, using the **Share** button. These include Safari, Contacts and the Mail app.

Notifications

The Notification Center option provides a single location to view all of your emails, messages, updates and alerts. It appears at the top right-hand corner of the screen. The items that appear in Notifications are set up within System Preferences. To do this:

1 Open System Preferences and click on the **Notifications** button

Notifications

2 The items that will appear in the Notification Center are listed here. Click on an item to select it and set its notification options

Notifications can be accessed regardless of the app in which you are working, and they can be actioned directly without having to leave the current app.

118

Twitter and Facebook feeds can also be set up to appear in the Notification Center, if you have accounts with these sites.

3 To disable an item so that it does not appear in the Notification Center, select it as above and check off the **Show in Notification Center** box

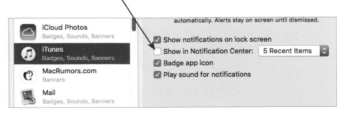

...cont'd

Viewing Notifications

Notifications appear in the Notification Center. The way they appear can be determined in the System Preferences:

 Select an alert style. A banner alert comes up on the screen and then disappears after a few seconds

2 The **Alerts** option shows the notification and it stays on screen until dismissed (such as this one for reminders)

3 Click on this button in the top right-hand corner of the screen to view all of the items in the Notification Center. Click on it again to hide the Notification Center

4 In the Notification Center, click on the **Today** button to view the weather forecast, calendar events and stock market reports for the current day. Click on the **Edit** button to change the items that appear

5 Click on the **Notifications** button to view the items that have been selected for here. Items such as emails and iMessages can be replied to directly by clicking on them from within the Notifications section

Hot tip

The Notification Center can also be displayed with a trackpad or Magic Trackpad by dragging with two fingers from right to left, starting from the far right edge.

Don't forget

Software updates can also appear in the Notification Center, when they are available.

Getting Around with Maps

With the Maps app you need never again wonder about where a location is, or worry about getting directions to somewhere. Using Maps with OS X El Capitan, you will be able to do the following:

- Search maps from around the world

- Find addresses

- Find famous buildings or landmarks

- Find the locations of people in your Contacts app

- Get directions between different locations

- View traffic conditions

Viewing maps

Enable **Location Services** and then you can start looking around maps, from the viewpoint of your current location.

Location Services can be enabled in **System Preferences > Security & Privacy**. Click on the **Privacy** tab, click on **Location Services** and check on the **Enable Location Services** checkbox. Maps can be used without Location Services but this would mean that Maps cannot use your current location or determine anything in relation to this.

  Click on this button on the Dock or in the Launcher

  Click on this button to view your current location

  Double-click to zoom in on a map. Alt + double-click to zoom out. Or, swipe outwards with thumb and forefinger to zoom in, and pinch inwards to zoom out

Or, click on these buttons to zoom in and out on a map

...cont'd

Finding locations

Locations in Maps can be found for addresses, cities or landmarks.
To find items in Maps:

1 Enter an item into the Search box and click on one of the results

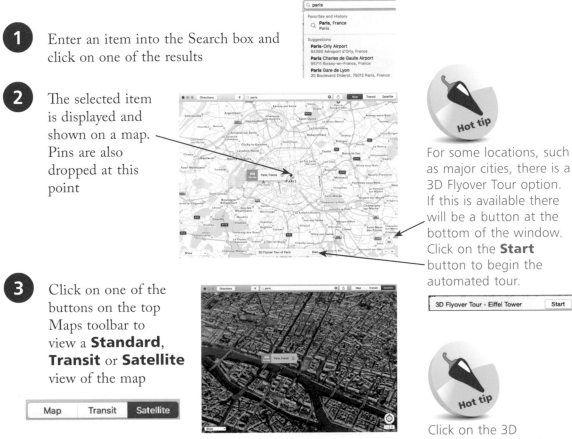

2 The selected item is displayed and shown on a map. Pins are also dropped at this point

3 Click on one of the buttons on the top Maps toolbar to view a **Standard**, **Transit** or **Satellite** view of the map

4 Click on the pin on the map to view its location

5 Click here to view more details about the location, including options for adding it to contact information and getting directions to the location. You can also access a Flyover Tour of the location (if available)

Hot tip

For some locations, such as major cities, there is a 3D Flyover Tour option. If this is available there will be a button at the bottom of the window. Click on the **Start** button to begin the automated tour.

3D Flyover Tour - Eiffel Tower	Start

Hot tip

Click on the 3D button to change the perspective of the map being viewed. Rotate your fingers on the trackpad to change the orientation of the map.

...cont'd

Getting directions

Within Maps you can also get directions to almost any location.

1 Click on the **Directions** button

Directions

Click on this button in Step 2 to swap the locations for which you want directions.

2 By default, your current direction is used for the **Start** field. If you want to change this, click once and enter a new location

Directions
Start: **Petrin Lookout Tower**
End: **Atmosferas**
Drive Walk Transit

3 Enter an **End** location or address

Click on the **Walk** button in Step 2 to view the directions by foot instead of car.

4 Click on one of the options for reaching your destination. The route is shown on the map, with the directions down the left-hand side of the window. The default mode of transport is for driving

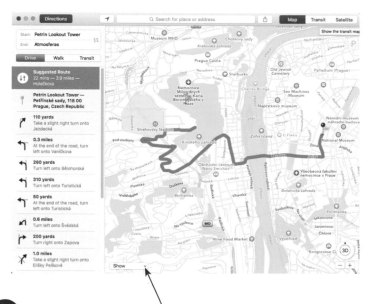

Click on the **Share** button to send the directions to a mobile device, such as an iPhone or an iPad, so that you can follow the directions on the go.

5 Click on **Show** button to view the map in 3D or for Traffic, which shows any traffic disruption

Finding transit directions

In OS X El Capitan there is an option for accessing transit options between two locations. To do this:

1 Enter the two locations, as shown on the previous page. Click on the **Transit** button

2 The transit options are shown in the left-hand panel

Hot tip

Click on the **Leaving Soon** box in Step 1 to specify a time for when your journey will be taking place. The transit details will be provided for your leaving time.

3 Click on the **Details** button next to an option to view its full details. This will include any parts of the journey where you will have to walk between the transit services required for your journey

Don't forget

The Transit option is only available for a limited number of locations around the world, the majority being in the US.

123

Preview

Preview is an OS X app that can be used to view multiple file types, particularly image file formats. This can be useful if you just want to view documents without editing them in a dedicated app, such as an image editing app. Preview in OS X El Capitan can also be used to store and view documents in iCloud.

1 Open Preview and click on one of the options in the Finder sidebar. This includes a link to Preview, but other locations can be used too

2 Double-click on an item to view it at full size. This can be from any of the folders within the Finder

124

Printing

OS X El Capitan makes the printing process as simple as possible, partly by being able to automatically install new printers as soon as they are connected to your Mac. However, it is also possible to install printers manually. To do this:

1 Open **System Preferences** and click on the **Printers & Scanners** button

Printers & Scanners

2 Currently installed printers are displayed in the Printers List. Click here to add a new printer

$+$

3 Select an available printer

Name
Dell Laser Printer 1720dn

4 Click on the **Add** button to load the printer drivers for the selected printer

Add

5 The printer drivers are added

Setting up 'Dell Laser Printer 1720dn...'

Setting up the device...

Configure   Cancel

6 The printer is added in the **Printers & Scanners** window, ready for use

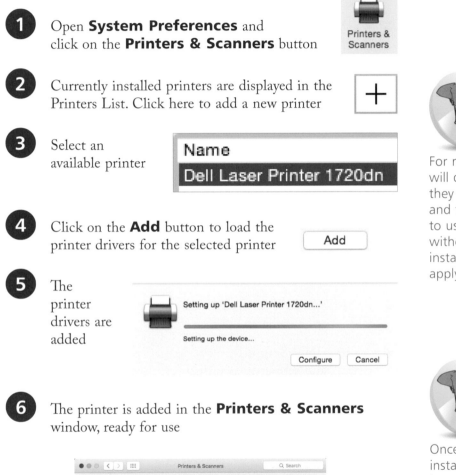

For most printers, OS X will detect them when they are first connected and they should be ready to use immediately, without the need to install any software or apply new settings.

125

Once a printer has been installed, documents can be printed by selecting **File > Print** from the Menu bar. Print settings can be set at this point and they can also be set by selecting **File > Page/Print Setup** from the Menu bar in most apps.

OS X Utilities

In addition to the apps in the Applications folder, there are also a number of utility apps that perform a variety of tasks within OS X. (Some of the utilities vary depending on the hardware setup of your Mac.) To access the Utilities:

Don't forget

The Utilities folder is also available from within the Applications folder.

 Access the Launchpad to access the Utilities folder. The utilities are displayed within the Utilities folder

- **Activity Monitor**. This contains information about the system memory being used and disk activity (see page 180 for more details).

- **AirPort Utility**. This sets up the AirPort wireless networking facility that can be used to connect to the internet with a Wi-Fi connection.

- **Script Editor**. This can be used to create your own scripts with Apple's dedicated scripting app, AppleScript.

- **Audio MIDI Setup**. This can be used for adding audio devices and setting their properties.

- **Bluetooth File Exchange**. This determines how files are exchanged between your computer and other Bluetooth devices (if this function is enabled).

- **Boot Camp Assistant**. This can be used to run Windows operating systems on your Mac.

- **ColorSync Utility**. This can be used to view and create color profiles on your computer. These can then be used by apps to try to match output color with monitor color.

- **Console**. This displays the behind-the-scenes messages that are being passed around the computer while its usual tasks are being performed.

Don't forget

You may never need to use a utility like the Console, but it is worth having a look at it just to see the inner workings of a computer.

- **DigitalColor Meter**. This can be used to measure the exact color values of a particular color.

- **Disk Utility**. This can be used to view information about attached disks and repair errors.

- **Feedback Assistant**. This can be used to send Apple feedback about the performance of OS X and also the in-built Apple apps. You have to sign-in with an Apple ID to use the Feedback Assistant and this will be same one used to create your iCloud account.

- **Grab**. This is a utility which can be used to capture screen shots, which are images of the screen at a given point in time. You can grab different portions of the screen, including a timed option, and even menus. The resultant images can be saved into different file formats.

- **Grapher**. This is a utility for creating simple or more complex scientific graphs.

- **Keychain Access**. This deals with items such as passwords when they are needed for networking. These do not have to be set but it can save time if you have to enter passwords on a lot of occasions. It also ensures that there is greater security for items protected by passwords.

- **Migration Assistant**. This helps in the transfer of files between two Mac computers. This can be used if you buy a new Mac and you need to transfer files from another one.

- **System Information**. This contains details of the hardware devices and software applications that are installed on your computer (see page 179 for more details).

- **Terminal**. This is used as an entry point into the world of UNIX. Within the Terminal you can view the workings of UNIX and also start to write your own apps, if you have some UNIX programming knowledge.

- **VoiceOver Utility**. This has various options for how the VoiceOver function works within OS X. This is the digital voice that can be used to read out what is on the screen and it is particularly useful for users who are visually impaired.

The Grab utility is useful if you are producing manuals or books and need to display examples of a screen or app.

127

The utilities are the workhorses of OS X. They do not have the glamour of apps such as iTunes but they perform vital information gathering and general maintenance tasks.

Creating PDF Documents

PDF (Portable Document Format) is a file format that preserves the formatting of the original document and it can be viewed on a variety of computer platforms including Mac, Windows and UNIX. OS X has a built-in PDF function that can produce PDF files from many apps. To do this:

PDF files can be viewed with the Preview app.

1 Open a file in an app and select **File > Export as PDF**

2 Browse to a destination for the file and click **Save**

PDF is an excellent option if you are creating documents such as instruction booklets, magazines or manuals.

3 Look in the selected location to view the newly created PDF file

luzu3

7 Internet and Email

This chapter shows how to get the most out of the internet and email. It covers connecting to the internet and how to use the OS X web browser, Safari, and its email app, Mail. It also covers Messages for text messaging, with audio and photos, and FaceTime for video and audio chatting.

Getting Connected

Connecting to the internet with a Mac is done through the System Preferences. To do this:

1 Click on the **System Preferences** icon on the Dock

2 Click on the **Network** icon

3 Check that your method of connecting to the internet is active, i.e. colored green

4 Click on the **Assist me...** button to access wizards for connecting to the internet with your preferred method of connection

Assist me...

5 Click on the **Assistant...** button

Assistant...

6 The **Network Setup Assistant** is used to configure your system so that you can connect to the internet
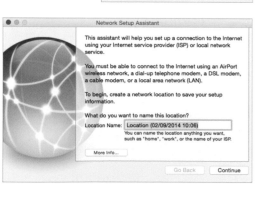

7 Enter a name for your connection

Location Name: Home Wi-Fi

8 Click on the **Continue** button   Continue

9 Select an option for how you will connect to the internet, e.g. wireless, cable or telephone modem

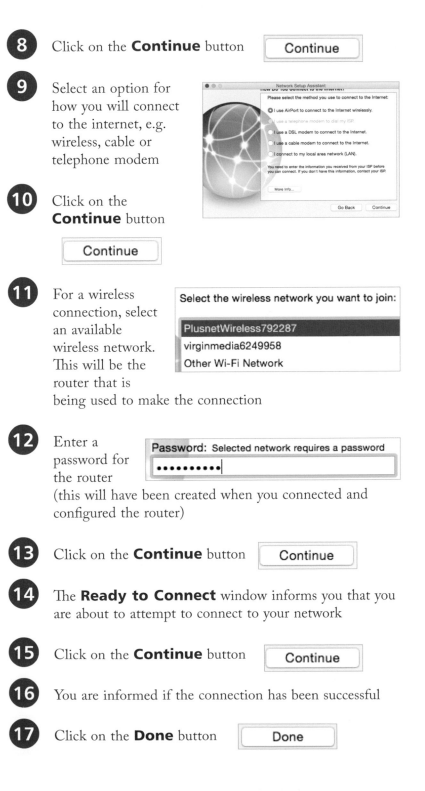

10 Click on the **Continue** button

Continue

11 For a wireless connection, select an available wireless network. This will be the router that is being used to make the connection

Select the wireless network you want to join:

PlusnetWireless792287

virginmedia6249958

Other Wi-Fi Network

12 Enter a password for the router

Password: Selected network requires a password

•••••••••

(this will have been created when you connected and configured the router)

13 Click on the **Continue** button   Continue

14 The **Ready to Connect** window informs you that you are about to attempt to connect to your network

15 Click on the **Continue** button   Continue

16 You are informed if the connection has been successful

17 Click on the **Done** button   Done

Hot tip

If you have an iPhone you can use your Mac and OS X El Capitan to create a Personal Hotspot, so that you can use the cellular Wi-Fi connection from your iPhone, if you cannot use your own Wi-Fi connection. To do this, both devices have to be signed in to the same iCloud account. Click on the Wi-Fi icon at the right-hand side of the top Menu bar and select your iPhone from the Wi-Fi menu. This will give you online access and you can reconnect to the Hotspot the next time that you want to use it, as long as your iPhone is near your Mac.

Safari

Safari is a web browser that is designed specifically to be used with OS X. It is similar in most respects to other browsers, but it usually functions more quickly and works seamlessly with OS X.

Safari overview

 Click here on the Dock to launch Safari

 All of the controls are at the top of the browser

Toolbar   Address/Search Bar   Tabs

Favorites Bar   Main content area

Address Bar/Search Box

In Safari, the Address Bar and the Search Box can be used for searching for an item or entering a web address to go to that page:

1 Click in the Address Bar/Search Box

2 Select an item from the Favorites page that appears, or enter a web address or search item into the box. Options will be displayed below the Address Bar/ Search Box

Safari Sidebar

A useful feature in Safari in OS X El Capitan is the Safari sidebar. This is a panel in which you can view all of your Bookmarks, Reading List items and Shared Links from social networking sites such as Twitter and LinkedIn.

1 Select **View > Show Sidebar** from the Safari Menu bar or click on this button

2 Click on the **Bookmarks** button to view all of the items that you have bookmarked. Click on the plus symbol **+** at the bottom of the sidebar panel to add more folders for your bookmarks

3 Click on the **Reading List** button to view all of the items that you have added to your reading list so that they can be read later, even if you are offline and not connected to the internet. These can be added from the **Share** button

4 Click on the **Shared Links** button to view items that have been posted by your contacts on sites such as Twitter and LinkedIn

Hot tip

Links to social networking accounts can be set up in **System Preferences > Internet Accounts**. Select the required account and enter the details with which you log in to it. Updates will then be available in the Shared Links panel of the sidebar.

Safari Tabbed Browsing

Tabs are now a familiar feature on web browsers, so you can have multiple sites open within the same browser window:

Safari is a full screen app and can be expanded by clicking the double arrow in the top right corner. For more information on full screen apps, see pages 98-99.

134

 When more than one tab is open, the tabs appear at the top of the web pages

 Click on this button next to the tabs to open a new tab

 Click on one of the **Top Sites** (see next page) or enter a website address in the Address Bar

 Click on this button next to the New Tab button to minimize all of the current tabs

5 Move left and right to view all of the open tabs in thumbnail view. Click on one to view it at full size

Select **Safari > Preferences** from the Menu bar to specify settings for the way Safari operates.

Safari Top Sites

Within Safari there is a facility to view a page showing thumbnails of the websites that you visit most frequently. This can be done from a button on the Safari Menu bar. To do this:

 Click on this button to view the **Top Sites** window

 The Top Sites window contains thumbnails of the websites that you have visited most frequently with Safari

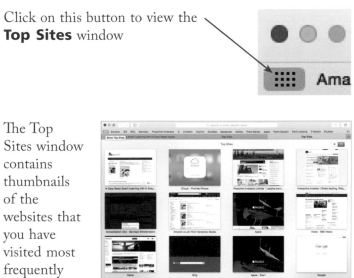

(this builds up as you visit more sites)

 Move the cursor over a thumbnail and click on the cross to delete a thumbnail from the **Top Sites** window. Click on the pin to keep it there permanently

In Easy Steps Smart Learning with In Easy...

 Click on a thumbnail to go to the full site

The Top Sites window is also accessed automatically as a landing page if you open a new tab within Safari.

Top Sites can also be added by opening the **sidebar** and dragging a bookmarked site into the Top Sites window.

Safari Reader

Web pages can be complex and cluttered things at times. On occasion, you may want to just read the content of one story on a web page without all of the extra material in view. In Safari this can be done with the Reader function. To do this:

Beware

Not all web pages support the Reader functionality in Safari.

Hot tip

Pages that are saved to a Reading List with the button in Step 6 can be read when you are offline, so you do not need to be connected to the internet.

1 Select **View > Show Reader** from the Safari Menu bar

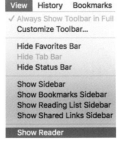

2 Click on the **Reader** button in the Address Bar of a web page that supports this functionality

3 The button turns black once the Reader is activated

4 The content is displayed in a text format, with a minimum of formatting from the original page

Thinkstock

Rapid diagnostic tests are urgently needed to help doctors know which patients need antibiotics, a report says.

The Review on Antimicrobial Resistance calls for tests to indentify viral and bacterial infections.

Only bacterial infections respond to antibiotics.

The review team said such tests could end "just in case" prescribing which sees a huge proportion of antibiotics used needlessly.

The review was set up last year by the Prime Minister David Cameron, who warned the world risked being plunged back into the Dark Ages of medicine by the overuse of antibiotics.

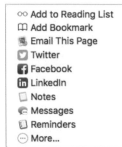

Don't forget

Other options can also be accessed from the **Share** button.

oo Add to Reading List
📖 Add Bookmark
📧 Email This Page
🐦 Twitter
📘 Facebook
in LinkedIn
📝 Notes
💬 Messages
🔖 Reminders
⋯ More...

5 Click on the **Share** button on the Safari toolbar if you want to save a page to read later

6 Click on this button to add the page to your Reading List

Adding Bookmarks

Bookmarks is a feature by which you can create quick links to your favorite web pages or the ones you visit most frequently. Bookmarks can be added to a menu or the Bookmarks sidebar in Safari which makes them even quicker to access. Folders can also be created to store the less frequently used bookmarks. To view and create bookmarks:

1 Click on this button to view the sidebar

2 Click on this button to view the bookmarks. All of the saved bookmarks can be accessed from here

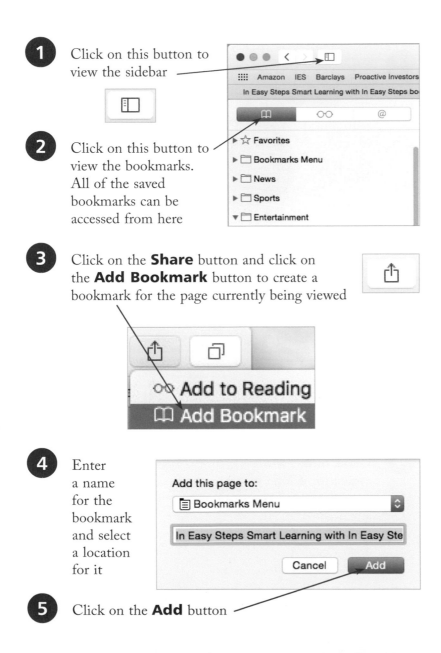

3 Click on the **Share** button and click on the **Add Bookmark** button to create a bookmark for the page currently being viewed

4 Enter a name for the bookmark and select a location for it

Add this page to:

📑 Bookmarks Menu

In Easy Steps Smart Learning with In Easy Ste

Cancel   Add

5 Click on the **Add** button

Beware

Only keep your most frequently used bookmarks in the Bookmarks sidebar, otherwise some of them will cease to be visible, as there will be too many entries for the available space.

Mail

Email is an essential element for most computer users and Macs come with their own email app called Mail. This covers all of the email functionality that anyone could need.

When first using Mail you have to set up your email account. This can be done with most email accounts and also a wide range of web mail accounts, including iCloud. To add email accounts:

Don't forget

Mail is a full screen app. For more information on full screen apps, see pages 98-99.

138

Don't forget

You can set up more than one account in the Mail app and you can download messages from all of the accounts that you set up.

1 Click on this icon on the Dock

2 Check on the button next to the type of account that you want to create. If you have an Apple ID you will already have an iCloud email address which can be entered

Choose a Mail account provider...

- ● iCloud
- ○ E⊠ Exchange
- ○ Google
- ○ YAHOO!
- ○ Aol.
- ○ Other Mail Account...

Cancel   Continue

3 Enter details of the account and click on the **Sign In** button

Sign in to use your Apple ID.
If you have an Apple ID, sign in with it here. If you have used the iTunes Store or iCloud, for example, you have an Apple ID. If you don't have an Apple ID, click Create Apple ID.

Apple ID   Password   Forgot?
nickvandome@mac.com   ••••••••

Create Apple ID   Cancel   Sign In

4 Check on the **Mail** option for iCloud to sync your iCloud email across any other Apple devices and also your online account at **www.icloud.com**

☁ iCloud

Account: nickvandome@mac.com

Use with:
- ☑ iCloud Drive
- ☐ Photos
- ☑ Mail
- ☑ Contacts
- ☑ Calendars
- ☑ Reminders

Cancel   Go Back   Add Account

Using Mail

Mail enables you to send and receive emails and also format them to your own style. This can be simply formatting text or adding customized stationery. To use Mail:

1 Click on the **Get Mail** button to download available email messages

2 Click on the **New Message** button to create a new email

3 Click on the **Format** button to access options for formatting the text in the email

4 Click on these buttons to **Reply** to, **Reply** (to) **All** or **Forward** an email you have received

5 Select or open an email and click on the **Delete** button to remove it

6 Click on the **Junk** button to mark an email as junk or spam. This trains Mail to identify junk mail. After a period of time, these types of messages will automatically be moved straight into the Junk mailbox

7 Click on the **Attach** button to browse your folders to include a file in your email. This can be items such as photos, Word documents or PDF files

8 Use these buttons in the New Message window to select fonts and font size, color, bold, italic, underlining, strikethrough and alignment options

Hot tip

To show the body text underneath an icon in Mail, Ctrl + click next to an icon and select **Icon & Text** from the menu.

Hot tip

When entering the name of a recipient for a message, Mail will display details of matching names from the Contacts app. For instance, if you type DA, all of the entries in your Contacts beginning with this will be displayed and you can select the required one.

Hot tip

If you Forward an email with an attachment then the attachment is included. If you Reply to an email, the attachment will not be included.

Mail in Full Screen

Since email is something that is often used on a regular basis, the Mail app has been enhanced in OS X El Capitan so that it has greater functionality when used in full screen mode.

 Open the Mail app and click on the green **Expand** button to view it in full screen mode

 Create an email using the **New Message** button and click on the orange **Minimize** button to save it as a draft

> To: Eilidh ˅
>
> Cc:
>
> Subject: **Next outing**
>
> From: Nick Vandome – nickvandome@me.com

Don't forget

The tabs function for draft emails is remembered if you toggle between full screen mode and standard mode.

 All draft emails are shown as tabs at the bottom of the window. Click on one to make it active

 When a new message is created, any other drafts are shown as tabs at the top of the window

...cont'd

5 As more drafts are created, they are added as tabs along the top of the active email window

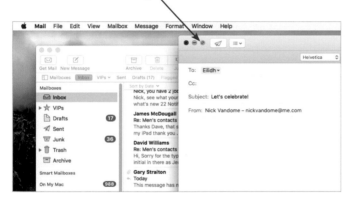

6 Individual messages can also be made full screen and worked on separately from the main email viewer. To do this, click on the green **Expand** button within a new message window

Don't forget

When an individual email message is made full screen, the main mail viewer (including your Inbox) remains in standard mode.

141

7 The new message window is displayed at full screen mode. Move the cursor over the top of the window to access the control buttons. Click on the orange **Minimize** button to return to standard mode

To: Eilidh

Cc:

Subject: **Let's celebrate!**

From: Nick Vandome – nickvandome@me.com

Messaging

The Messages app enables you to send text messages (iMessages) to other OS X El Capitan users or those with an iPhone, iPad or iPod Touch using iOS 5 or later. It can also be used to send photos, videos and make FaceTime calls. To use Messages:

1 Click on this icon on the Dock

2 You require an Apple ID to use Messages and you will need to enter these details when you first access it. If you do not have an Apple ID you will be able to create one at this point

3 Click on this button to start a new conversation

4 Click on this button and select a contact (these will be from your Contacts app). To send an iMessage, the recipient must have an Apple ID

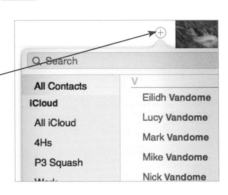

5 The person with whom you are having a conversation is displayed in the left-hand panel

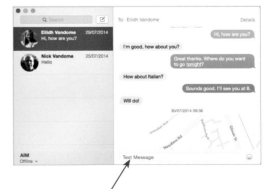

6 The conversation continues down the right-hand panel. Click here to write a message and press **Return** to send

...cont'd

Adding photos and videos

Photos and videos can be added to messages:

1 Select the photo or video in the Finder, next to the Messages app

2 Drag the photo or video into the text box to include it in a message

Text forwarding

If you have an iPhone you can receive and send SMS text messages, using your Mac with OS X El Capitan. To use your Mac to send and receive SMS messages:

1 On your Mac, from the Messages top Menu bar click on **Messages > Preferences > Accounts**. Click on the **iMessages** account tab and check **On** your own phone number and email address

2 On your iPhone, select **Settings > Messages > Send & Receive** and add your email address

3 On your iPhone, select **Settings > Messages > Text Message Forwarding > Turn Text Message Forwarding On**

4 An activation code appears on your Mac; enter this on your iPhone to enable text forwarding

Hot tip

Audio messages can also be included in an iMessage. Click on this icon to the right of the text box and record your message.

Don't forget

To use text forwarding you need to have OS X Yosemite (or later) on your Mac and iOS 8.1 (or later) on your iPhone, or iPad with cellular capabilities, i.e. the 3/4G version. Wi-Fi also has to be turned on for each device.

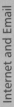
FaceTime

FaceTime is an app that can be used to make video and audio calls to other Macs, iPhones, iPads and iPod Touches. To use FaceTime on your Mac you must have an in-built FaceTime camera or use a compatible external one. To use FaceTime:

Don't forget

If you receive a video call, you are alerted to this even if FaceTime is not open and running.

 Click on this icon on the Dock

 You need an Apple ID to use FaceTime. Enter your details and click on the **Sign in** button

144

Hot tip

In a similar way to text forwarding, OS X El Capitan on a Mac can also be used for Phone Call Forwarding with your iPhone. Both devices need to have Wi-Fi turned on and be signed into the same iCloud account. On your Mac, select **FaceTime > Preferences >** and turn **On iPhone Cellular Calls**. Do the same on your iPhone with **Settings > FaceTime > iPhone Cellular Calls**. When you receive a call, it shows up as a notification on your Mac and you can Accept or Decline it.

Once you have logged in you can make video calls by selecting people from your address book providing they have an Apple ID, and a device that supports FaceTime. Click on this button to access your address book

(8) Digital Lifestyle

Leisure time, and how we use it, is a significant issue for everyone. This chapter details some of the options with OS X El Capitan, including the Photos app and Apple Music.

146

Using the Photos App

For a number of years the photo management and editing tool for OS X has been iPhoto. However, in Spring 2015 the Photos app was introduced. iPhoto can still be used, but the Photos app is designed to mirror the one used on iOS 9 devices and integrate more with iCloud, so that you can store all of your photos in the iCloud and then view and manage them on each of your Apple devices.

If you are using the Photos app, you can specify how it operates with iCloud in the iCloud System Preferences:

1 Click on the **System Preferences** button

2 Click on the **iCloud** button in the System Preferences window

3 Check On the **Photos** checkbox

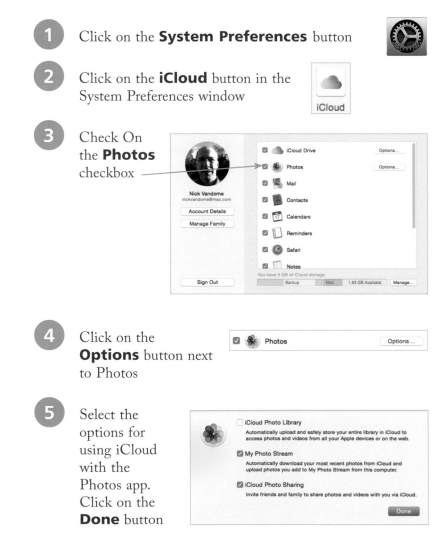

4 Click on the **Options** button next to Photos

5 Select the options for using iCloud with the Photos app. Click on the **Done** button

Viewing Photos

The Photos app can be used to view photos according to Years, Collections, Moments or at full size. This enables you to view your photos according to dates and times at which they were taken.

1 Click on these buttons at the top of the Photos window to move between Years, Collections and Moments

2 Click on the left-hand button in Step 1 to move to **Years** view

3 Click and hold on a thumbnail in Years view to enlarge it

4 Click on a photo within the Years section to view the **Collections**. This displays groups of photos (Moments) taken at the same location

...cont'd

Don't forget

Click on the **Photos** tab at the top of the Photos app window to view your photos in **Years**, **Collections**, **Moments** or full size.

Don't forget

Drag this slider to change the magnification of the photo, or photos, being displayed, in Moments, or at full size view.

Hot tip

Roll over a photo in Collections or Moments view and click on the left-hand icon below to view the relevant photos as a slideshow.

5 Click on a photo within the Collections section to view specific **Moments**. This displays photos taken at the same time in the same location

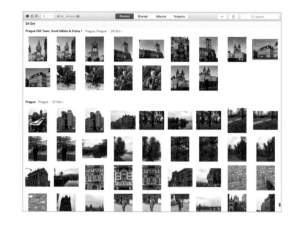

6 Double-click on a photo in the Collections or Moments section to view it at full size

7 For a photo being displayed at full size use these buttons, from left to right, to: add it as a favorite, view information about it, add a new album and create items, share the photo or edit it

Editing Photos

The Photos app has a range of editing options that can be used to enhance your photos. To do this:

1 Open a photo at full size

2 Click on the **Edit** button

Edit

3 The editing options are displayed at the right-hand side of the screen. Click on one to access its specific settings

4 Some editing options, such as **Filters**, have a one-click option for applying the effect. Others, such as **Adjust**, have a range of panels which can be used to make specific editing changes, such as to the light or color of a photo. Some of these panels also have an **Auto** option

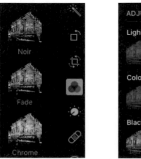

Don't forget

Click on the **Done** button at the top of the Photos app window to apply any editing changes that have been made. Click on the **Revert to Origina**l to discard the changes (this can also be done when you return to a photo that has been edited).

Revert to Original   Done

Starting with iTunes

Music is one of the areas that has revived Apple's fortunes in recent years, primarily through the iPod music player and iTunes, and also the iTunes music store, where music can be bought online. iTunes is a versatile app but its basic function is to play a music CD. To do this:

1 Click on this button on the Dock and insert the CD in the CD/DVD drive

2 By default, iTunes will open and display this window. Click **No** if you just want to play the CD

Would you like to import the CD "The Best Of Vivaldi" into your iTunes library?

☐ Do not ask me again

No   Yes

3 Click on the CD name in the sidebar and double-click on a track to play it, or

The Best Of Vivaldi

Hot tip

Notifications can be set to display each iTunes item as it is being played. To do this, ensure **iTunes** is selected in **Notifications** within **System Preferences**. Access the Notifications (see page 119) and the currently playing item will be displayed.

4 Click on this button to play a track or a whole CD

5 Click on the **Import CD** button if you want to copy the music from the CD onto your hard drive

Import CD

Buying Music with iTunes

As well as copying music from CDs into iTunes, it is also possible to download a vast selection of music from the iTunes online store. To do this:

1 Click on the **iTunes Store** link to access the online store

2 Navigate around the iTunes Store using panels and sections within the iTunes Store homepage

3 To find a specific item, enter the details in the **Search** box at the top right-hand corner of the iTunes window

4 Select an item, and details are displayed within the Store. Click on the price button to buy and download the track or album. This will appear in the **My Music** section of the iTunes app

Beware

Never use illegal music download sites. Apart from the legal factor, they are much more likely to contain viruses and spyware.

To buy music from the iTunes Store you must have an Apple ID and a linked credit or debit card for purchases.

151

Click on the **Music** button in the iTunes window to select different genres to view.

Using Apple Music

Apple Music is a new service that makes the entire Apple iTunes library of music available to users. It is a subscription service, but there is a 3-month free trial. Music can be streamed over the internet or downloaded so you can listen to it when you are offline. To start with Apple Music:

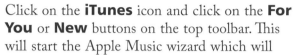

1 Click on the **iTunes** icon and click on the **For You** or **New** buttons on the top toolbar. This will start the Apple Music wizard which will start your free 3-month trial and also ask for some music preferences so that the service can be tailored for you

2 Click on the **For You** or **New** buttons on the top toolbar to view suggested playlists or specific tracks. These can all be played directly using streaming over Wi-Fi

To end your Apple Music subscription at any point (and to ensure you do not subscribe at the end of the free trial) open **iTunes** and select **Store > View Account** from the top Menu bar. Log in with your Apple ID and select **Account Info**. Under **Settings** click on **Subscriptions > Manage**. Click on the **Edit** button and drag the **Automatic Renewal** button to **Off**. You can then renew your Apple Music membership, if required, by selecting one of the **Renewal Options**.

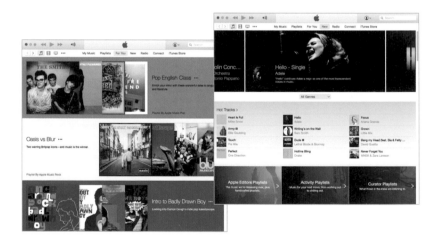

3 Click on individual items to view their details

...cont'd

4 Click next to a track or album to access menu options. These include adding it to your own **My Music** section in iTunes, where it can also be played if you are offline, by clicking on the cloud icon next to it

5 Click on the **My Music** button on the top toolbar to view all items here, including those that have been bought from the iTunes Store. The most recent items appear at the top of the window

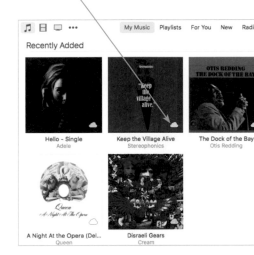

6 Click on items within the **My Music** section to view them. Click on an item to play it

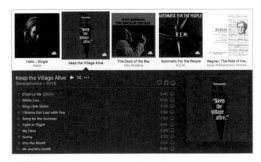

7 The currently playing item is displayed at the top of the iTunes window where they can be managed with the music controls

Numerous radio stations can also be listened to with Apple Music, including Beats 1.

153

Click on the **Connect** button on the top toolbar to select artists to follow so that you get the latest music information and updates about them.

Reading with iBooks

iBooks is an ebook reading app that has been available with Apple's mobile devices, including the iPhone and the iPad, for a number of years. OS X El Capitan also offers this technology to desktop and laptop Macs. To use iBooks:

1 Click on this icon on the Dock or within the Launchpad

2 Click on the **Get Started** button

3 Click on the **Sign In** button to sign in with your Apple ID and access the iBooks Store

4 If you are signed in with your Apple ID, click on the **iBooks Store** button

5 The iBooks Store contains a wide range of books that can be previewed and downloaded

6 Click on a title to preview details about it

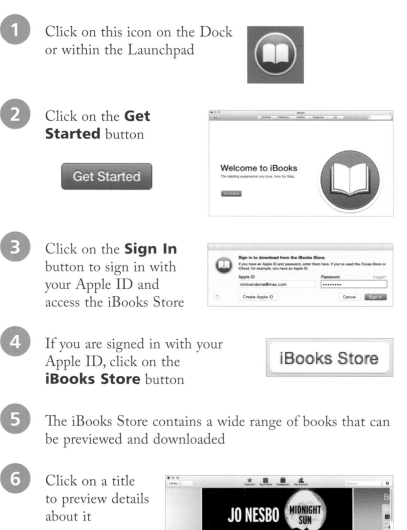

...cont'd

7 Click here to download the book (if it is a paid-for title this button will display a price)

From the iBooks Store, click on the **Library** button in the top left-hand corner to go back to your own Library.

8 The title will be downloaded into your iBooks Library. Double-click on the cover to open the book and start reading

Use these buttons on the top toolbar of a book to, from left to right, go back to your Library, view the table of contents or view any notes you have added.

9 Click or tap on the right-hand and left-hand edges to turn a page. Move the cursor over the top of the page to access the top toolbar. The bottom toolbar displays the page numbers and location

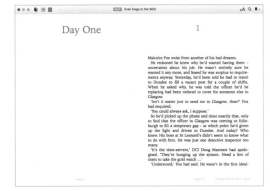

Use these buttons on the top toolbar to, from left to right, change the page appearance, search for text and add a bookmark to a page.

Movies, Music and Games

With OS X El Capitan, your Mac really can become your own personal entertainment center. In addition to photos, music and books, there is also a range of apps that can be used to create your own movies, make music and play games. These can all be accessed in the **Applications** folder or from the **Launchpad**.

iMovie

This is an app that can be used to create your own home movies. You can download footage from your video camera or smartphone and then edit it in iMovie. Numerous features can be added, including transitions between scenes, text, music, voiceovers and special effects.

Other apps for creating movies and music can also be downloaded from the App Store.

DVDs

In the past, Apple produced an app called iDVD for creating artistic presentations from your own home movies. However, this has now been discontinued, but other DVD-creation apps can be obtained in the App Store.

GarageBand

For anyone who wants to create their own music, this is the ideal app. There is a wide range of pre-set loops that can be used to build up music tracks, and you can also select different instruments and create your own tracks by playing the onscreen keyboard which generates the music for the selected instrument.

Game Center

This app gives access (with an Apple ID) to an environment where you can not only play your favorite games and download more from the App Store, but also compare your scores and achievements against other Game Center players. It is also possible to compete directly against other people in multi-player games, where you can both play the same game simultaneously.

9 Sharing OS X

This chapter looks at how to set up and manage different user accounts on your Mac.

Adding Users

OS X enables multiple users to access individual accounts on the same computer. If there are multiple users, i.e. two or more, for a single machine, each person can sign on individually and access their own files and folders. This means that each person can log in to their own settings and preferences. All user accounts can be password protected, to ensure that each user's environment is secure. To set up multiple user accounts:

Don't forget

Every computer with multiple users has at least one main user, also known as an administrator. This means that they have greater control over the number of items that they can edit and alter. If there is only one user on a computer, they automatically take on the role of the administrator. Administrators have a particularly important role to play when computers are networked together. Each computer can potentially have several administrators.

Don't forget

Each user can select their own icon or photo of themselves.

1 Click on the **System Preferences** icon on the Dock

2 Click on the **Users & Groups** icon

3 The information about the current account is displayed. This is your own account and the information is based on details you provided when you first set up your Mac

4 Click on this icon to enable new accounts to be added (the padlock needs to be open)

Click the lock to prevent further changes.

5 Click on the plus sign icon to add a new account

6 Enter the details for the new account holder

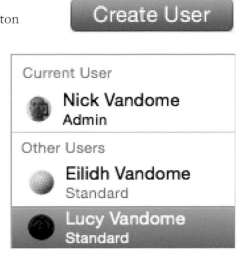

New Account: Standard

Full Name: Lucy Vandome

Account Name: lucyvandome
This will be used as the name for your home folder.

Password: ○ Use iCloud password
● Use separate password

••••••   ♀

••••••

Online

?   Cancel   Create User

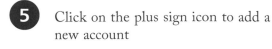

By default, you are the administrator of your own Mac. This means that you can administer other user accounts.

159

7 Click on the **Create User** button

Create User

8 The new account is added to the list in the Accounts window, under **Other Users**

Current User

Nick Vandome
Admin

Other Users

Eilidh Vandome
Standard

Lucy Vandome
Standard

Deleting Users

Once a user has been added, their name appears on the list in the Accounts preference dialog box (see Step 3 on page 158). It is then possible to edit the details of a particular user or delete them altogether. To do this:

 Within **Users & Groups**, select a user from the list

Current User

Nick Vandome
Admin

Other Users

Eilidh Vandome
Standard

Lucy Vandome
Standard

 Click here to remove the selected person's user account

—

3 A warning box appears to check if you really do want to delete the selected user. If you do, select the required option and click **OK**

Are you sure you want to delete the user account "Lucy Vandome"?

To delete this user account, select what you want to do with the home folder for this account, and then click "Delete User".

● Save the home folder in a disk image
The disk image is saved in the Deleted Users folder (in the Users folder).

○ Don't change the home folder
The home folder remains in the Users folder.

○ Delete the home folder
☐ Erase home folder securely

Cancel   Delete User

160

Fast User Switching

If there are multiple users using OS X it is useful to be able to switch between them as quickly as possible. When this is done, the first user's session is retained so that they can return to it if required. To switch between users:

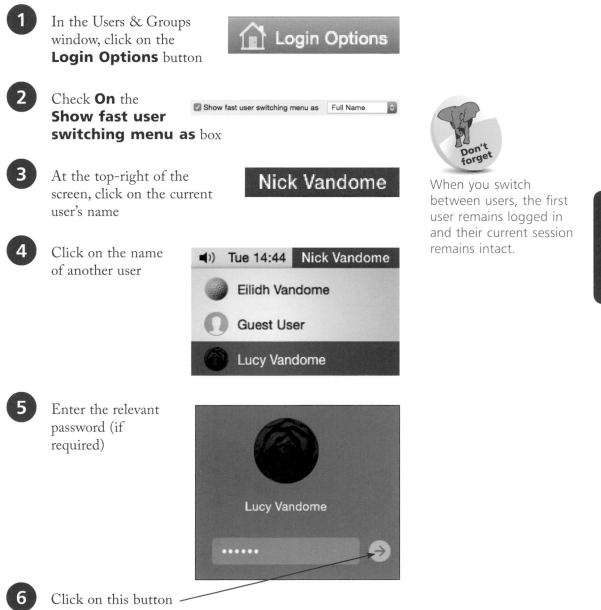

1 In the Users & Groups window, click on the **Login Options** button

🏠 Login Options

2 Check **On** the **Show fast user switching menu as** box

☑ Show fast user switching menu as   Full Name ⌄

3 At the top-right of the screen, click on the current user's name

Nick Vandome

4 Click on the name of another user

◀)) Tue 14:44   Nick Vandome
🏌 Eilidh Vandome
🧑 Guest User
🌹 Lucy Vandome

5 Enter the relevant password (if required)

Lucy Vandome
•••••• →

6 Click on this button to log in

Don't forget

When you switch between users, the first user remains logged in and their current session remains intact.

Parental Controls

If children are using the computer, parents may want to restrict access to certain types of information that can be viewed, using Parental Controls. To do this:

1 Access **Users & Groups** and click on a username. Check **On** the **Enable parental controls** box and click on the **Open Parental Controls...** button

☑ Enable parental controls   Open Parental Controls...

Hot tip

To check which sites have been viewed on a web browser, check the History menu, which is located on the main Menu bar.

2 Click on the **Apps** tab   Apps

3 Check **On** this box if you want to limit the types of app that a user can access

 ☑ Limit Applications on this Mac
Allow the user to open only the specified applications on this Mac. An administrator password is required to open other applications.

Allowed Apps: 🔍 Search

▼ ☑ Other Apps
  ☑ 🅰 AAM Updates Notifier
  ☑ 📇 Adobe Bridge CS4
  ☑ 📖 Adobe Elements 9 Organizer
  ☑ ℹ️ Adobe Help.app

4 Under **Allowed Apps**, check **Off** the boxes next to the apps that you do not want used

5 Click here to select options for using the Game Center and also limiting emails to allowed contacts (click on the **Manage** button to specify allowed contacts)

☑ Allow joining Game Center multiplayer games
☑ Allow adding Game Center friends

☑ Limit Mail to allowed contacts   Manage...

...cont'd

Web controls

1 Click on the **Web** tab

2 Check **On** this button to try to prevent access to websites with adult content

3 Check **On** this button to specify individual websites that are suitable to be viewed

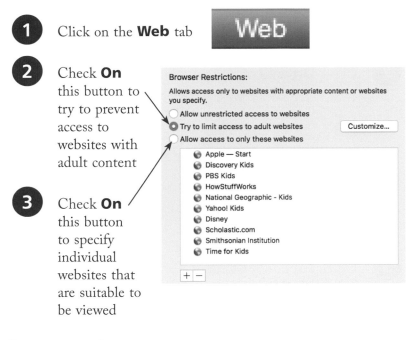

Browser Restrictions:
Allows access only to websites with appropriate content or websites you specify.

○ Allow unrestricted access to websites
◉ Try to limit access to adult websites   [Customize...]
○ Allow access to only these websites

- 🌐 Apple — Start
- 🌐 Discovery Kids
- 🌐 PBS Kids
- 🌐 HowStuffWorks
- 🌐 National Geographic - Kids
- 🌐 Yahoo! Kids
- 🌐 Disney
- 🌐 Scholastic.com
- 🌐 Smithsonian Institution
- 🌐 Time for Kids

[+ | −]

Stores controls

1 Click on the **Stores** tab

2 Check **On** the items under **Disable** that you do not want available and apply the necessary settings under **Restrict**, in terms of types of content that is permissible

Disable: ☑ iTunes Store
☐ iTunes U
☐ iBooks Store

Restrict: ☑ Music with explicit content
☐ Movies to: [12 ⬍]
☐ TV shows to: [CAUTION ⬍]
☑ Apps to: [12+ ⬍]
☑ Books with explicit sexual content

Hot tip

If you are setting Web controls for a child, or grandchild, discuss this with them too so they understand what you are doing and why. This could also be a good time to discuss some of the issues of online security, such as never replying to any type of message or contact from people you do not know.

...cont'd

Time controls

1 Click on the **Time** tab

2 Check **On** this box to limit the amount of time the user can use the Mac during weekdays

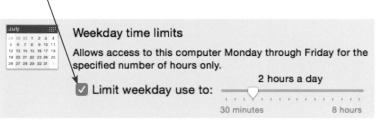

3 Check **On** this box to limit the amount of time the user can use the Mac during weekends

4 Check **On** these boxes to determine the times at which the user cannot access their account

10 Networking

This chapter looks at networking and how to share files over a network.

Networking Overview

Before you start sharing files directly between computers, you have to connect them together. This is known as networking and can be done with two computers in the same room, or with thousands of computers in a major corporation. If you are setting up your own small network it will be known in the computing world as a Local Area Network (LAN). When setting up a network there are various pieces of hardware that are initially required to join all of the required items together. Once this has been done, software settings can be applied for the networked items. Some of the items of hardware that may be required include:

- **A network card**. This is known as a Network Interface Card (NIC) and all recent Macs have them built in.

- **A wireless router**. This is for a wireless network which is increasingly the most common way to create a network, via Wi-Fi. The router is connected to a telephone line and the computer then communicates with it wirelessly.

- **An Ethernet port and Ethernet cable**. This enables you to make the physical connection between devices. Ethernet cables come in a variety of forms, but the one you should be looking for is the Cat5E type as this allows for the fastest transfer of data. If you are creating a wireless network then you will not require these.

- **A hub**. This is a piece of hardware with multiple Ethernet ports that enables you to connect all of your devices together and lets them communicate with each other. However, conflicts can occur with hubs if two devices try to send data through one at the same time.

- **A switch**. This is similar in operation to a hub but it is more sophisticated in its method of data transfer, thus allowing all of the machines on the network to communicate simultaneously, unlike a hub.

Once you have worked out all of the devices that you want to include on your network, you can arrange them accordingly. Try to keep the switches and hub within relative proximity of a power supply and, if you are using cables, make sure they are laid out safely.

Hot tip

If you have two Macs to be networked and they are in close proximity then this can be achieved with an Ethernet crossover cable. If you have more than two computers, then this is where an Ethernet hub is required. In either case, there is no need to connect to the internet to achieve the network.

Ethernet network

The cheapest and easiest way to network computers is to create an Ethernet network. This involves buying an Ethernet hub or switch, which enables you to connect several devices to a central point, i.e. the hub or switch. All Apple computers and most modern printers have an Ethernet connection, so it is possible to connect various devices, not just computers. Once all of the devices have been connected by Ethernet cables, you can then start applying network settings.

AirPort network

Another option for creating a network is using Apple's own wireless system, AirPort. This creates a wireless network and there are two main options used by Apple computers: AirPort Express, using the IEEE 802.11n standard, which is more commonly known as Wi-Fi, which stands for Wireless Fidelity, and the newer AirPort Extreme, using the next generation IEEE 802.11ac standard which is up to five times faster than the 802.11n standard. Thankfully, AirPort Express and Extreme are also compatible with devices based on the older IEEE standards, 802.11b/g/n, so one machine loaded with AirPort Extreme can still communicate wirelessly with the older AirPort version.

One of the main issues with a wireless network is security, since it is possible for someone with a wireless-enabled machine to access your wireless network if they are within range. However, in the majority of cases the chances of this happening are fairly slim, although it is an issue about which you should be aware.

The basic components of a wireless network between Macs is an AirPort card (either AirPort Express or AirPort Extreme) installed in all of the required machines, and an AirPort base station that can be located anywhere within 150 meters of the AirPort enabled computers. Once the hardware is in place, wireless-enabled devices can be configured by using the AirPort Setup Assistant utility found in the Utilities folder. After AirPort has been set up, the wireless network can be connected. All of the wireless-enabled devices should then be able to communicate with each other, without the use of a multitude of cables.

Wireless network

A wireless network can also be created with a standard wireless router, rather than using the Airport option.

Don't forget

Another method for connecting items wirelessly is called Bluetooth. This covers much shorter distances than AirPort and is usually used for items such as printers and smartphones. Bluetooth devices can be connected by using the Bluetooth Setup Assistant in the Utilities folder.

Network Settings

Once you have connected the hardware required for a network, you can start applying the network settings that are required for connecting to the internet, for online access.

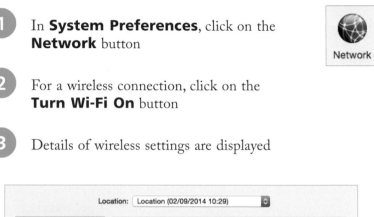

1 In **System Preferences**, click on the **Network** button

2 For a wireless connection, click on the **Turn Wi-Fi On** button

3 Details of wireless settings are displayed

An Ethernet cable can be used to connect to a router instead of using a Wi-Fi connection and it can also be used to connect two computers.

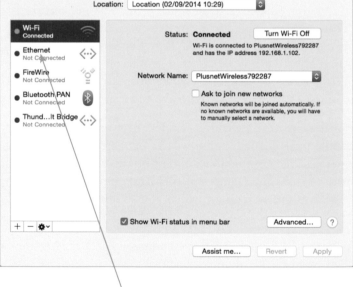

4 For a cable connection, connect an Ethernet cable and click on the **Ethernet** button

5 Click on the **Advanced...** button to see the full settings for each option

Advanced...

File Sharing

One of the main reasons for creating a network of two or more computers is to share files between them. On networked Macs, this involves setting them up so that they can share files, and then accessing these files.

Setting up file sharing
To set up file sharing on a networked Mac:

 Click on the **System Preferences** button on the Dock

 Click on the **Sharing** icon

 Check **On** the boxes next to the items you want to share (the most common items to share are files and printers)

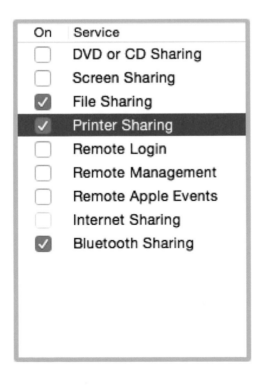

Hot tip

For OS X El Capitan users, files can also be shared with the AirDrop option. This can be used with two Macs and compatible iPhones and iPads that have this facility. When it is accessed, files can be shared simply by dragging them onto the icon of the other user that appears in the AirDrop window. To access AirDrop, click on this button in the Finder.

Beware

If no file sharing options are enabled in the **Sharing** preference window, no other users will be able to access your computer or your files, even on the network.

Connecting to a Network

Connecting as a registered user

To connect as a registered user (usually as yourself when you want to access items on another one of your own computers):

Don't forget

You can disconnect from a networked computer by ejecting it in the Finder in the same way as you would for a removable drive such as a DVD.

1 Other connected computers on the network will show up in the Shared section in the Finder. Click on a networked computer

Shared

🖴 Mac-00254...

2 Click on the **Connect As...** button

Connect As...

3 Check on the **Registered User** button and enter your username and password

Enter your name and password for the server "Mac-00254bb4190e".

Connect as: ⚪ Guest
⚫ Registered User
⚪ Using an Apple ID

Name: nickvandome

Password: ●●●●●●●

☐ Remember this password in my keychain

Change Password...   Cancel   Connect

4 Click on the **Connect** button

5 The public folders and home folder of the networked computer are available to the registered user. Double-click on an item to view its contents

Connected as: nickvandome

Name

▦ Eilidh Vandome's Public Folder
▦ Lucy Vandome's Public Folder
▦ Macintosh HD
▦ Nick Vandome's Public Folder
▦ nickvandome

...cont'd

See page 186 for further details.

Guest users

Guest users on a network are users other than yourself, or other registered users, to whom you want to limit access to your files and folders. Guests only have access to a folder called the Drop Box in your own Public folder. To share files with Guest users you have to first copy them into the Drop Box. To do this:

1 Create a file and select **File > Save** from the Menu bar

2 Navigate to your own home folder (this is created automatically by OS X and displayed in the Finder Sidebar)

3 Double-click on the **Public** folder

4 Double-click on the **Drop Box** folder

5 Save the file into the Drop Box

Beware

If another user is having problems accessing the files in your Drop Box, check the permissions settings that have been assigned to the files. See page 186 for further details.

Hot tip

The contents of the Drop Box can be accessed by other users on the same computer as well as users on the network.

Beware

The Drop Box folder is not the same as the Dropbox app, which is used for online storage and backing up.

...cont'd

Accessing a Drop Box

To access files in a Drop Box:

Beware

It is better to copy files into the Drop Box rather than moving them completely from their primary location.

Hot tip

Set permissions for how the Drop Box operates by selecting it in the Finder and Ctrl + clicking on it. Select **Get Info** from the menu and apply the required settings under the **Sharing & Permissions** heading.

1 Double-click on a networked computer in the Finder

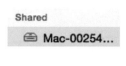
Shared
Mac-00254...

2 Click on the **Connect As...** button in the Finder window

Connect As...

3 Check on the **Guest** button

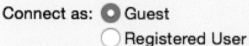
Connect as: ○ Guest
○ Registered User
○ Using an Apple ID

4 Click on the **Connect** button

Connect

5 Double-click on a user's **Public** folder

Nick Vandome's Public Folder

6 Double-click on the **Drop Box** folder to access the files within it

Drop Box

11 Maintaining OS X

Despite its stability, OS X still benefits from a robust maintenance regime. This chapter looks at ways to keep OS X in top shape, ensure downloaded apps are as secure as possible and some general troubleshooting.

Time Machine

Time Machine is a feature of OS X that gives you great peace of mind. In conjunction with an external hard drive, it creates a backup of your whole system, including folders, files, apps and even the OS X operating system itself.

Once it has been set up, Time Machine takes a backup every hour and you can then go into Time Machine to restore any files that have been deleted or become corrupt.

Setting up Time Machine

To use Time Machine it first has to be set up. This involves attaching a hard drive to your Mac. To set up Time Machine:

Make sure that you have an external hard drive that is larger than the contents of your Mac, otherwise Time Machine will not be able to back it all up.

1 Click on the **Time Machine** icon on the Dock or access it in System Preferences

2 You will be prompted to set up Time Machine

Your Time Machine backup disk can't be found.

Cancel | Set Up Time Machine

3 Click on the **Set Up Time Machine** button

Set Up Time Machine

4 In the Time Machine System Preferences window, click on the **Select Disk...** button

Select Disk...

5 Connect an external hard drive and select it from the Available Disks list

6 Click on the **Use Disk** button

7 In the Time Machine System Preferences window, drag the button to the **On** position

Time Machine
OFF [ ] ON

When you first set up Time Machine it copies everything on your Mac. Depending on the type of connection you have for your external drive, this could take several hours. Because of this, it is a good idea to have a hard drive with a Firewire connection to make it as fast as possible.

8 The backup will begin. The initial backup copies your whole system and can take several hours. Subsequent hourly backups only look at items that have been changed since the previous backup

Time Machine
130 GB of 250 GB available
Oldest backup: Today, 15:48
Latest backup: Today, 15:48
Next backup: Today, 16:15
Select Disk...

If you stop the initial backup before it has been completed, Time Machine will remember where it has stopped and resume the backup from this point.

9 The progress of the backup is displayed in the System Preferences window and also here

Backup Complete
Time Machine has finished the first backup to "Time Machine".
Close

...cont'd

Using Time Machine

Once the Time Machine has been set up it can then be used to go back in time to view items in an earlier state. To do this:

1 Access an item on your Mac and delete it. In this example, the folder **iMac** has been deleted

2 Click on the **Time Machine** icon

3 The Time Machine displays the current item in its current state (the iMac folder is deleted). Earlier versions are stacked behind it

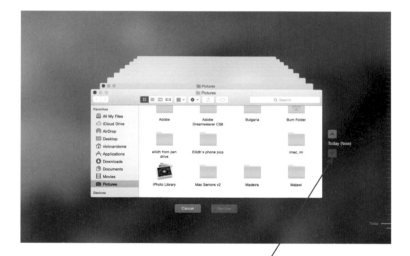

4 Click on the arrows to move through the open items or select a time or date from the scale to the right of the arrows

5 Another way to move through the Time Machine is to click on the pages behind the first one. This brings the selected item to the front

Beware

If you have deleted items before the initial set up of Time Machine, these will not be recoverable.

Don't forget

The hard drive must be connected in order to use Time Machine.

Don't forget

The active item that you were viewing before you launch Time Machine is the one that is active in the Time Machine interface. You can select items from within the active window to view their contents.

…cont'd

 6 Click on the **Restore** button to restore any items that have been deleted (in this case the iMac folder)

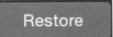

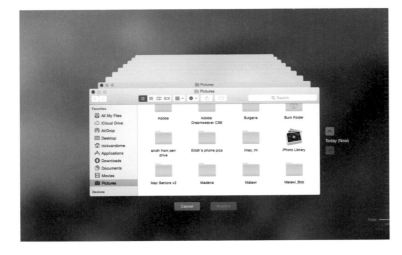

Don't forget

Items are restored from the Time Machine backup disk, i.e. the external hard drive.

7 Click on the **Cancel** button to return to your normal environment

Cancel

8 The deleted folder **iMac** is now restored to its original location

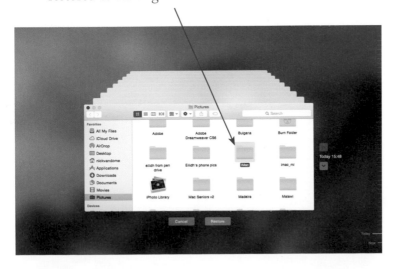

Disk Utility

Disk Utility is a utility app that allows you to perform certain testing and repair functions for OS X. It incorporates a variety of functions and it is a good option for both general maintenance and if your computer is not running as it should.

Each of the functions within Disk Utility can be applied to specific drives and volumes. However, it is not possible to use the OS X start-up disk within Disk Utility as this will be in operation to run the app, and Disk Utility cannot operate on a disk that has apps already running. To use Disk Utility:

Checking disks

Don't forget

Disk Utility is located within the **Applications > Utilities** folder.

1 Click the **First Aid** tab to check a disk

2 Select a disk and select one of the first aid options

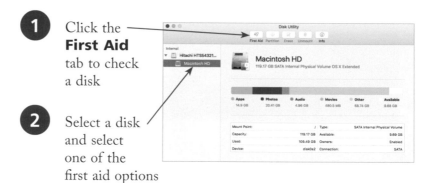

Erasing a disk

To erase all of the data on a disk or a volume:

Don't forget

If there is a problem with a disk and OS X can fix it, the **Repair** button will be available. Click on this to enable Disk Utility to repair the problem.

1 Click on the **Erase** tab and select a disk or a volume

Beware

If you erase data from a removable disk, such as a pen drive, you will not be able to retrieve it.

2 Click **Erase** to erase the data on the selected disk or volume

System Information

This can be used to view how the different hardware and software elements on your Mac are performing. To do this:

 Open the **Utilities** folder and double-click on the **System Information** icon

 Click on the **Hardware** link and click on an item of hardware

▼ Hardware
  ATA
  Audio
  Bluetooth
  Camera
  Card Reader
  Diagnostics
  Disc Burning

System Information is located within the **Applications > Utilities** folder.

Details about the item of hardware, and its performance, are displayed

MATSHITA DVD-R   UJ-898:

```
Firmware Revision:  HE13
Interconnect:       ATAPI
Burn Support:       Yes (Apple Shipping Drive)
Cache:              1024 KB
Reads DVD:          Yes
CD-Write:           -R, -RW
DVD-Write:          -R, -R DL, -RW, +R, +R DL, +RW
Write Strategies:   CD-TAO, CD-SAO, DVD-DAO
Media:              To show the available burn speeds, insert a disc and
                    choose File > Refresh Information
```

 Similarly, click on software items to view their details

Calendar	8.0

Calendar:

```
Version:          8.0
Obtained from:    Apple
Last Modified:    16/09/2015, 16:17
Kind:             Intel
64-Bit (Intel):   Yes
Signed by:        Software Signing, Apple Code Signing Certification
                  Authority, Apple Root CA
Location:         /Applications/Calendar.app
```

Activity Monitor

Activity Monitor is a utility app that can be used to view information about how much processing power and memory is being used to run apps. This can be useful to know if certain apps are running slowly or crashing frequently. To use Activity Monitor:

Activity Monitor is located within the **Applications > Utilities** folder.

Activity Monitor

 1 Click on the **CPU** tab to see how much processor capacity is being used up

System:	1.03%	CPU LOAD	Threads:	719
User:	0.45%		Processes:	187
Idle:	98.51%			

 2 Click on the **Memory** tab to see how much system memory (RAM) is being used up

MEMORY PRESSURE		Physical Memory:	8.00 GB	App Memory:	1.90 GB
		Memory Used:	2.94 GB	Wired Memory:	1.04 GB
		Cached Files:	1.30 GB	Compressed:	0 bytes
		Swap Used:	0 bytes		

 3 Click on the **Disk** tab to see how much space has been taken up on the hard drive

Reads in:	86,144	IO ⌄	Data read:	2.65 GB
Writes out:	20,518		Data written:	530.0 MB
Reads in/sec:	0		Data read/sec:	0 bytes
Writes out/sec:	1		Data written/sec:	8.80 KB

Updating Software

Apple periodically releases updates for its software; both its apps and the OS X operating system. All of these are now available through the App Store. To update software:

1 Open **System Preferences** and click on the **App Store** icon

App Store

2 Click here to select options for how you are notified about updates and how they are downloaded

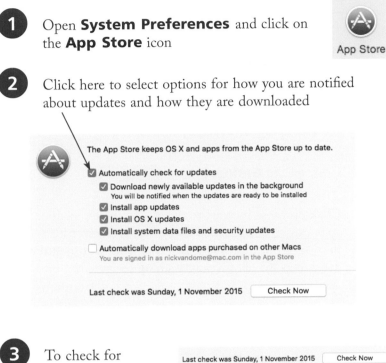

3 To check for updates manually, click on the **Check Now** button

Last check was Sunday, 1 November 2015   Check Now

4 Available updates are shown in the Updates section in the App Store. Click on the **Update** buttons to update. If there are no updates available this will be stated, with the latest updates underneath

181

Software updates can also be accessed directly from the Apple menu, located on the top Menu bar. If updates are available this is denoted by a number on the **App Store** link on the Apple menu.

Check **On** the **Automatically download apps purchased on other Macs** box if you want to activate this function.

For some software updates, such as those to OS X itself, you may have to restart your computer for them to take effect.

Gatekeeper

Internet security is an important issue for every computer user; no-one wants their computer to be infected with a virus or malicious software. Historically, Macs have been less prone to attack from viruses than Windows-based machines, but this does not mean Mac users can be complacent. With their increasing popularity there is now more temptation for virus writers to target them. OS X El Capitan recognizes this and has taken steps to prevent attacks with the Gatekeeper function. To use this:

1 Open **System Preferences** and click on the **Security & Privacy** button

Security & Privacy

2 Click on the **General** tab   General

3 Click on these buttons to determine which locations apps can be downloaded from. You can select from just the Mac App Store, or Mac App Store and identified developers, which gives you added security in terms of apps having been thoroughly checked, or from anywhere

Allow apps downloaded from:
- ○ Mac App Store
- ◉ Mac App Store and identified developers
- ○ Anywhere

4 Under the **General** tab there are also options for using a password when you log in to your account and also if a password is required after sleep or if the screen saver is activated

A login password has been set for this user   Change Password...

☑ Require password [immediately ⌄] after sleep or screen saver begins

☐ Show a message when the screen is locked   Set Lock Message...

☐ Disable automatic login

Privacy

Also within the Security & Privacy System Preferences are options for activating a firewall and privacy settings. To access these:

1 Click on the **Firewall** tab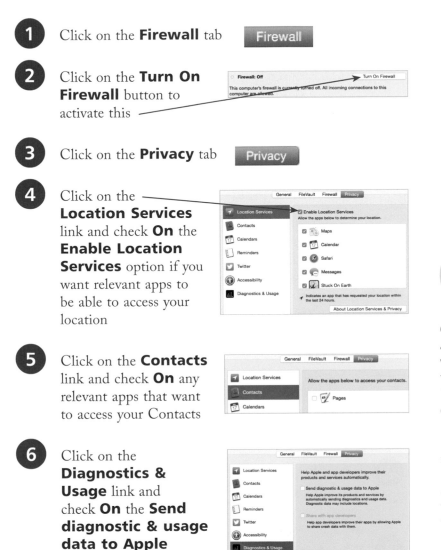

2 Click on the **Turn On Firewall** button to activate this

3 Click on the **Privacy** tab

4 Click on the **Location Services** link and check **On** the **Enable Location Services** option if you want relevant apps to be able to access your location

5 Click on the **Contacts** link and check **On** any relevant apps that want to access your Contacts

6 Click on the **Diagnostics & Usage** link and check **On** the **Send diagnostic & usage data to Apple** if you want to send information to Apple about the performance of your Mac and its apps. This will include any problems, and helps Apple improve its software and apps. This information is collected anonymously and does not identify anyone personally

OS X El Capitan apps are designed to do only what they are supposed to, so that they do not have to interact with other apps if they do not need to. This lessens the possibility of any viruses spreading across your Mac. For instance, only apps that have the ability to use Contacts will ask for permission to do this.

Problems with Apps

The simple answer

OS X is something of a rarity in the world of computing software: it claims to be remarkably stable, and it is. However, this is not to say that things do not sometimes go wrong, although this is considerably less frequent than with older Mac operating systems. Sometimes this will be due to problems within particular apps and on occasions the problems may lie with OS X itself. If this does happen, the first course of action is to close down OS X using the **Apple menu > Shut Down** command. Then, restart the computer. If this does not work, or you cannot access the Shut Down command, try turning off the power to the computer and then starting up again.

Force quitting

If a particular app is not responding, it can be closed down separately without the need to reboot the computer. To do this:

Beware

When there are updates to OS X these can, on rare occasions, cause issues with some apps. However, these are usually fixed with subsequent patches and upgrades to OS X.

1 Select **Apple menu > Force Quit** from the Menu bar

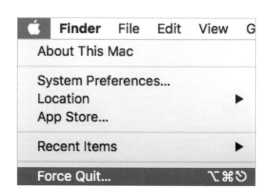

2 Select the app you want to close

3 Click **Force Quit**

General Troubleshooting

It is true that things do occasionally go wrong with OS X, although probably with less regularity than with some other operating systems. If something does go wrong, there are a number of areas that you can check and also some steps you can take to ensure that you do not lose any important data if the worst case scenario occurs, and your hard drive packs up completely:

- **Backup**. If everything does go wrong it is essential to take preventative action in the form of making sure that all of your data is backed up and saved. This can be done with either the Time Machine app or by backing up manually by copying data to a CD or DVD. Some content is also automatically backed up if you have iCloud activated.

- **Reboot**. One traditional reply by IT helpdesks is to reboot, i.e. turn off the computer and turn it back on again and hope that the problem has resolved itself. In a lot of cases this simple operation does the trick, but it is not always a viable solution for major problems.

- **Check cables**. If the problem appears to be with a network connection or an externally connected device, check that all cables are connected properly and have not become loose. If possible, make sure that all cables are tucked away so that they cannot be inadvertently pulled out.

- **Check network settings**. If your network or internet connections are not working, check the network setting in System Preferences. Sometimes when you make a change to one item this can have an adverse effect on one of these settings. (If possible, lock the settings once you have applied them, by clicking on the padlock icon in the Network preferences window.)

- **Check for viruses**. If your computer is infected with a virus this could affect the efficient running of the machine. Luckily this is less of a problem for Macs as virus writers tend to concentrate their efforts towards Windows-based machines. However, this is changing as Macs become more popular and there are plenty of Mac viruses out there. So make sure your computer is protected by an app such as Norton AntiVirus which is available from **www.norton.com**

Don't forget

In extreme cases, you will not be able to reboot your computer normally. If this happens, you will have to pull out the power cable and re-attach it. You will then be able to reboot, although the computer may want to check its hard drive to make sure that everything is in working order.

...cont'd

- **Check Start-up items**. If you have set certain items to start automatically when your computer is turned on, this could cause certain conflicts within your machine. If this is the case, disable the items from launching during the booting up of the computer. This can be done within the Accounts preference of System Preferences by clicking on the **Startup Items** tab, selecting the relevant item and pressing the minus button.

- **Check permissions**. If you, or other users, are having problems opening items this could be because of the permissions that are set. To check these, select the item in the Finder, click on the **File** button on the top Menu bar and select **Get Info**. In the **Sharing & Permissions** section of the Info window you will be able to set the relevant permissions to allow other users, or yourself, to read, write or have no access.

Click here to view permissions settings

- **Eject external devices**. Sometimes external devices, such as pen drives, can become temperamental and refuse to eject the disks within them, or even show up on the Desktop or in the Finder at all. If this happens, you can eject the disk by pressing the mouse button when the Mac chimes are heard during the booting up process.

- **Turn off your screen saver**. Screen savers can sometimes cause conflicts within your computer, particularly if they have been downloaded from an unreliable source. If this happens, change the screen saver within the **Desktop & Screen Saver** preference of the System Preferences or disable it altogether.

If you are having problems opening a document that you have been sent from a trusted source, contact them to make sure that the document has not been locked with a password. If you receive documents from someone you do not know, such as by email, do not open them as they may contain viruses or malware.

186

Index